Property of GREGORY C POTTS

DAVID
After God's Own Heart

H. Edwin Young

BROADMAN PRESS
Nashville, Tennessee

© Copyright 1984 • Broadman Press
All rights reserved.
4215-31
Dewey Decimal Classification: 221.92
Subject heading: DAVID, KING OF ISRAEL
Printed in the United States of America

Library of Congress Cataloging in Publication Data

Young, H. Edwin.
  David, after God's own heart.

  1. David, King of Israel.   2. Palestine—Kings
and rulers—Biography.   3. Bible.   O.T.—Biography.
4. Bible.   O.T.   Samuel—Criticism, interpretation, etc.
I. Title.
BS580.D3Y68   1984   222'.40924 [B]   83-71873
ISBN 0-8054-1531-9

This book is dedicated to
my dear brother in Christ,
Cliff Barrows—
Without a doubt—a modern man
After God's Own Heart!

ACKNOWLEDGMENTS

For their assistance, I express grateful appreciation to the following people, who not only assisted in the preparation of this manuscript, but whose personal support and friendship have also been a ministry of encouragement in my life: Betty and Roy Brockman, Billie Jean Buckley, Lucy Carl, Angel Cope, Beverly Gambrell, Libby Kelton, Barry Landrum, Lisa Milne, Kathy Nelson, Linda Richard, Deedra Walton, and Cathy Wyatt.

Also, I must thank Vicki Phillips who forced me to clarify my muddy thinking in so many places. Without her tenacity, this book would have died prematurely.

Once again, my dear wife Jo Beth had the final word of approval. She cut through miles of ministerial verbiage and sharpened many phrases. She beautifully personifies the excellent wife described in Proverbs 31:10-31.

ED YOUNG
Houston, Texas

Preface

David: After God's Own Heart is an inspirational study of the
life of Israel's greatest king. From the sheepfold in the lonely hills,
God called this mystical man to become the sovereign from whose
lineage his own Son, the Lord Jesus Christ, was born. David was a
writer, a musician, a shepherd, a military genius. He loved God
and knew how to follow him. But like every human being, he had
that tragic flaw!

Study his life, and you will be touched by his humility; preach
from his story, and your church family will find principles for
keeping their priorities in order and their lives right with God.
From the backside of the mountain to the throne room of Israel,
David sang the praises of God. Through his words, he reached for
the Lord in an unparalleled manner. How the mighty have fallen!
But how this mighty man, though weak, was made strong through
the power of God!

David offers hope for the one who finds himself in the throes of
distress and heartache. God is the Lord of the repentant heart—
and he is still reaching, loving, convincing, and convicting. It is my
prayer that you will find examples from David's life which will help
you climb to greater heights with God. No classical or alliterative
outlines are used herein. As a general rule, the Scripture is dealt
with chronologically.

Contents

1
The Making of a Giant Killer

Psalm 78; 1 Samuel 13:10-15

He chose David also his servant, and took him from the sheep-folds (Ps. 78:70).

More is known about David than perhaps any other biblical personality. There are fourteen chapters in the Scripture given to Abraham. The chronicles of Joseph are also described in fourteen chapters. Jacob's story is told in eleven chapters; Elijah's, nine chapters. Sixty-six Bible chapters, with fifty-nine references in the New Testament, are given to David. More is recorded of his birth, childhood years, teenage years, adult years; more intimate minutiae about his family life, his reign, and literary skill than any other scriptural character.

With this much of the Bible given to his life and to the events which surrounded him, is it any surprise that he is called "a man after God's own heart"? But when we think of David, two events come to mind. First of all, we recall his battle with the giant, Goliath. The second event we remember is his involvement with Bathsheba: how he fell into the sins of murder and adultery. After these episodes, most of us are somewhat nebulous about this staggeringly important progenitor of Jesus.

David is a modern man. His life is unusually relevant for today. Study the life of the giant killer, and you will discover that the smallest giant he ever battled was Goliath. The other giants David tackled were much tougher and more deadly than the Philistine bully.

To understand this complex man, you have to encounter Saul, David's nemesis for ten years. First Samuel 8—13 tells of Saul's reign. He ruled capriciously until God announced through Samuel a devastating word of judgment.

> 13 *And Samuel said to Saul, Thou hast done foolishly: thou hast not kept the commandment of the Lord thy God, which he commanded thee: for now would the Lord have established thy kingdom upon Israel forever.* 14 *But now thy kingdom shall not continue: the Lord hath sought him a man after his own heart, and the Lord hath commanded him to be captain over his people, because thou hast not kept that which the Lord commanded thee"* (1 Sam. 13:13,14).

GRACE GROWS BEST IN WINTER

The choices we make determine the shape and the color of our lives. Many times I have stood at a crossroad. There is a road going to the left, a road to the right, and a road straight ahead. Sometimes as I have tried to decide what direction I should take, the clouds have opened; the sun has streamed through; the road markings have been clear, and twelve or fifteen godly friends have advised, "That's the way to go." I have had no problem going in that way. It seemed right and appropriate; it seemed to have the leadership of God about it.

Other times I have stood at a crossroad, and I have not been sure. There were crowds all around who wanted to push me down one path without my having any part in making the decision. Other times I have stood at a crossroad, and I have sought for direction from any source. I have gone out into open fields looking for any tracks which would give me a sense of the mind of God, and I couldn't even find rabbit tracks in the ground! No direction was evident.

Sometimes we come to a crossroad, and have a long time to consider the direction in which God would have us go. We want to choose what is best, what is good, what is moral, what is proper. We think about it, pray about it, get counsel about it, meditate on it, and read the Scripture steadily and unhurriedly. God's will becomes obvious. However, occasionally a crisis comes, and a decision must be made immediately. There is no time to delay. "I'm going to take this step. This is it—now or never." And we

DAVID: AFTER GOD'S OWN HEART

make a decision and act upon it. Now, if we have been drawing all of our strength from the Lord; and we have been seeking his best, his mind, and his heart, then in the moment of crisis, we will make the right decision!

But woe to the person who discovers the principles of God in a time of crisis. Mark it down: When a decision has to be made, *what* we know isn't very important; *Whom* we know is extremely important. The question is not, "Am I going in the right direction?" The question is, "Am I directed by the Director?" And if the Director has been calling the shots in my life, then I have the resources to meet the crisis when it comes. I can say, "Oh, Lord, you know I want your will, your way, your best in my life. Therefore, as I come to this juncture in the road, I move out authoritatively (even through the fog, the confusion of sickness, a wayward child, poverty, vocational difficulty, or whatever). I move out courageously because You are the foundation of my life." So many times we discover that *grace grows best in the winter*!

GILGAL AND BETHLEHEM

Saul and David walked together to the same intersection; they came to the same crossroad. One went one way; one went the other. But in the beginning, Saul and David were so much alike. Saul was from Gilgal; David, from Bethlehem—with similar roots. Consider how their lives ended. Today, Saul has been relegated to a dark place in biblical history. An appropriate title for his life story would be, "The Tragedy of a Self-made Man." David? Why, many people are named David! Over the King David Hotel in Jerusalem, his flag is flying; his star is resplendent. Jews and Christians alike wear the Star of David. It was in the lineage of David that our own Savior was born.

How important is a good start? Think back to your high school and college years. There was that guy who had it made: captain of the team; straight As; everything going his way. Years later we see an old friend and ask, "By the way, what happened to Joe? Do you know where he is?" And the reply comes, "Well, you know, all that potential, all that ability, all that talent, all that drive . . . he had everything. But . . . " Then the story varies, but we have all heard the tragic detours many times: a divorce never dealt with;

THE MAKING OF A GIANT KILLER 11

an addiction never faced; a moral problem never confessed; a vocational disaster never understood. The facts are so different, yet so much alike: a history of wrong choices; side streets; detours; running away from God, therefore running away from life. Sow an act; reap a habit. Sow a habit; reap a life-style. Sow a life-style; reap a destiny. How does it happen? Perhaps the first kings of Israel will help us understand.

David and Saul both were appointed by God and were anointed by God's prophet, Samuel. They felt the oil of Samuel going through their locks, down their necks, and their strong young backs as they were anointed king. Neither Saul nor David tried or dreamed or had any aspirations of being king. Saul became a king like George VI of England: by advocation. Never had he thought about it, but there he was—king! David? Samuel was visiting the house of Jesse, after God had declared that one of Jesse's boys would be the next king. Samuel looked at those seven stalwart sons of Jesse, straight and tall. But God's choice was not present. Finally, Samuel asked, "Are these all your boys?" And Jesse answered, "Well, you know, I've got one boy out there in the field. He's just a child who keeps the sheep. You aren't interested in him." "Ah," Samuel requested, "bring that boy to me." David came out of the field smelling like the sheep he attended. But God said to Samuel, "That's the one. David is the king." Perhaps the most unlikely second round draft pick in kingdom history! Then, the anointing oil of God flowed over his head and his body.

Saul and David were alike in their humility. When the time came for Saul's coronation service, he could not be found. They said, "Where's the man who would be the king?" He was hiding in the baggage, and they had to drag him out and make him king (1 Sam. 10:21 *ff*). Saul was condescending. As he was leaving, some went with him whose hearts God had touched. However, others made derogatory remarks; but wise Saul moved above all the clatter, because God had touched his life and selected him to be king.

David was so humble that even after he had been anointed, and after he had killed Goliath, he felt that he was unworthy to marry Saul's daughter, "I'm just a shepherd with a small flock of sheep.

DAVID: AFTER GOD'S OWN HEART

I'm not good enough to marry the king's daughter."

Both of these men began physically strong. The Bible records that Saul was a head taller than anyone else in Israel. He was a John Wayne! He was so tall that if he were living today, all the NBA scouts would be trying to get him under contract. The Bible says he was handsome. What about David? He was ruddy. That probably means he was red-headed, or blonde at least, and had piercing eyes. Both were athletically inclined, with some innate natural gifts. They were so alike at the beginning; but so different at the end.

A MATTER OF SIN

Thirty centuries later we reverence and study the life of David, but what happened to Saul? What is the difference? Consider the sins they committed. David's transgressions were grossly wicked. He was an unbelievable sinner. Saul's sin does not seem to be nearly as devastating. It seems surprising that David is noted as a man after the heart of God and that Saul is disgraced. What happened? What was the difference? When a crisis came, one made the right step; and one made the wrong step; and the end was a life-style.

Saul would make a misstep but instead of turning around, retracing his steps and trying to find directions, he simply blundered on down those steps into the basement! David would walk with God and then he would stumble, but he would receive directions from God and again climb the heights!

Once I was speaking in Bossier City, Louisiana. The weather was terrible: floods, tornadoes, rain, the worst possible conditions! I was anxious to jog. I finally decided to leave the motel and get some exercise in the misting rain. So, I ran through a little shopping area and crossed over the interstate in order to jog through a residential section. The streets were unmarked, and after having to turn around in a couple of cul-de-sacs, I had lost all sense of direction.

It was raining and cold, and I had jogged almost to exhaustion, but I just continued to push forward. Everywhere I ran, the dogs were getting larger and larger! Finally, I saw a truck coming down the road; nobody else was around because no one with any sense

THE MAKING OF A GIANT KILLER

would be out in such weather! I flagged down the guy and was comforted to see that he was from the city engineering department. He didn't know what was wrong with me, I'm sure. I explained, "Partner, I am lost. Where am I?" Fortunately, he carried me back to the motel.

If I had been like Saul, I would still be running around Bossier City! Saul would say, "I know where I'm going. I know the directions; I can just loop back over here and everything will be fine." He would become lost, and he would take another step as the situation worsened. He didn't know how to ask, "Where am I? Where should I be?" Never would he admit, "I'm lost; I want to go back; I want to begin again." Saul could not do that; David could! David would take all the pieces of his broken life and he would pray, "God, I give it back to you. Put it together again."

A MONSTER WITH GREEN EYES

Note how Saul stumbled and how he continually went down. His first misstep was that of *impatience*. He was lined up to fight the Philistines (1 Sam. 13). He was anxious to go to battle; he marshaled all of his troops. The Philistines were on the other side of the mountain. Samuel, the prophet of God, informed Saul, "I will be gone for seven days. When I come back, we will build an altar; we will offer the sacrifice, the peace offering, and the burnt offering to the Lord; and then we will fight the Philistines." Samuel left.

Saul moaned, "What a time for Samuel to leave!" One day went by, then two days. The troops were restless and ready to fight. Three days. Four days. Finally some began to desert. Saul was trying to keep them all together. The sixth day he reported, "Samuel is not here." The seventh day Saul said, "Well, I'll just put the wood together and get everything ready so when Samuel comes we can get this offering underway." Finally, on the seventh day, Saul said, "I will offer the sacrifice." He took the place of God's priest and offered the sacrifice. Just as he finished offering the sacrifice, in walked Samuel! The fire was still smoldering.

Samuel was a straightforward man. He looked at the king who held the power of life and death over him and declared, "Saul, you are a fool! Because of your impatience, and because you have

14   **DAVID: AFTER GOD'S OWN HEART**

presumed on God and his worship, the kingdom will be taken from you. Your children will not be heirs to the throne." And from that day on, Saul operated on his own ingenuity, his own strength, his own power, because the Spirit of God had departed from his life. Impatience was Saul's first step downhill.

The second step was that of *partial obedience* (1 Sam. 15). Because the Amalekites had not helped the Israelites when they had come out of Egypt, God commanded Saul and his army through Samuel, "Kill all the Amalekites—every person and every animal—and destroy everything they have." Saul went to battle. After he returned, the Bible tells us that he went on top of Mount Carmel, then back to Gilgal where he met Samuel. The first statement he made was, "Samuel, I have been obedient to the command of God. I have destroyed everything of the Amalekites." Samuel answered, "Is that right? What is that I'm hearing? What is that noise? Isn't that the bleating of the lamb? Isn't that the sound of the oxen I am hearing? What about all the animals? Where did they come from?"

Saul alibied, "Well, you know, we culled out the best animals and brought them to make a sacrifice to the Lord. And, oh, by the way, we did keep the king of the Amalekites. And we did save some of the gold because that's valuable property for the Lord." Saul always had an excuse when he was confronted with sin! He could always explain it away. Like Adam, he rationalized, "It's not me—it's Eve." Eve came back with, "Oh, you've got the wrong person. It's the snake."

Saul would shift the blame right on down the line! Then Samuel gave Saul a most important principle: *"To obey is better than sacrifice, and to hearken than the fat of rams"* (1 Sam. 15:22). What did he mean? Simply this: We can go to church, read the Bible, pray, memorize Scripture, recite all the Ten Commandments and all the Beatitudes, and be able to quote the Book of Revelation, but unless ours is a life-style of obedience to the will and the plan of God, all our sacrifice means nothing. Our worship is without significance. If we go to church to "do our duty" or to "feel good," or if we attend so we will have some little entree with God when crisis comes, then worship means nothing. Sacrifice flows from an obedient, submissive heart and mind. *Woe to the* person who has to learn the principles of God in the midst of a crisis! Partial obedience in God's accounting is disobedience. "Lord, I've almost fulfilled everything. Lord, I'm almost totally clean. Lord, I'm almost honest. I'm better than most people." Oh, no. God says, "I want all of you!"

Look at Saul's third step. He built a monument to himself on the top of Mount Carmel (1 Sam. 15:12). He defeated the Amalekites. He was partially obedient—then he built his own memorial. How different was David! This shepherd king never thought about a monument, except a monument to the Lord. In his heart, he wanted to build a Temple. He cried to the Lord, "Oh, God, I want to build a Temple. I want a place for your ark to be placed permanently." And he thought and dreamed and prayed and agonized over a Temple. The Temple was the only monument which interested David.

Saul was also disloyal. He was disloyal to David, his best friend and most effective soldier. Saul was even disloyal to his son, Jonathan. Saul said to his troops, "You're not to eat anything until evening comes" (1 Sam. 14:24 *ff.*). Jonathan had been fighting all day and did not know his father's command. He scooped up some honey on the end of his spear and ate it—and his eyes were brightened. He was strengthened. Saul would have killed Jonathan, his own son, because of an immoral oath—unknown to Jonathan—had not the army interceded. He was disloyal to friends and to family, to soldiers and supporters. He would do anything to build himself up. Does any of this sound familiar?

Saul's fourth downfall was jealousy. Remember when this green-eyed giant appeared? David had killed Goliath, and Saul was marching back from the battlefield victorious over the Philistines (1 Sam. 18). Then he heard some girls singing, "Saul hath killed his thousands, David hath killed his ten thousands." The song became a hit! Soldiers whistled it, girls sang it, and it went right to the top of the charts in Israel. Everybody was humming the tune and singing the words. And every time Saul heard it, he couldn't stand it! The Bible says from the time he first heard the song of praise to David, " . . . *Saul eyed David from that day on*" (1 Sam. 18:4, RSV). Jealousy overcame the king.

Usually, we are not jealous of someone older or younger than

DAVID: AFTER GOD'S OWN HEART

we. We are jealous of people who are in our same vocation: our peers. A woman is envious of another woman. "Look at her. She's so slim and trim and yet she eats like a horse! I drink water and eat lettuce and gain five pounds! It's not fair!" Then jealousy comes, and she says, "Well, she's probably not a good wife. She's not the cook I am! I don't think she really loves her children. She's not faithful to the church." After a close look at her life, we discover that in every area she seems to make an A-plus. Jealousy finds a stronghold.

When we belittle people, most of the time we are trying to bring them down to our level. The root cause most often is jealousy. Oh, we disguise it, we dress it up in costumes; we are very subtle about it. We even express it in the language of "piousity." I have heard more people slandered in prayer meeting than one can believe! Someone will spout off, "Oh, brethren, we need to pray for so-and-so and their trouble." And they proceed to explain all the sordid details.

AFTER GOD'S HEART

How swift we are at confessing another's sins and problems when they need loving and lifting up. They need quiet prayers uttered and friends who will rally around them in their distress. The great tragedy is that the Christian army far too often shoots its wounded! But what about David? How could David be a man after the heart of God when he sinned over and over? What did he have that Saul didn't have? One essential quality: *David knew how to repent.* Now, Saul knew the words. In 1 Samuel 15:27 Saul was before Samuel. Saul grabbed Samuel's legs, crying, "Oh Samuel, I'll offer the right offering; I confess my sin! Oh, Samuel, let me have your approval; let me get back to God!" Saul cried and agonized, but the real clue about Saul's relationship with the Lord is in one passage: 1 Samuel 15:15. Saul said, *"The Lord THY God"* (caps mine). He was Samuel's God, Samuel's Lord—not Saul's! We cannot claim the faith of another! The Lord must be *our* own personal God.

At those crucial times, David never had to find God's number in the phone book! He knew the number of his Friend! He had dialed it many times on those Judean hills, and he never had received a busy signal; God always answered David. When a crisis came, David knew how to talk with God. Saul would wrestle with problems, he would try to get through to God, he would talk with God, he would talk with God's man, Samuel, and then he would put God on hold! Is God on hold in your life? There is always a reason, a problem. "Somebody hurt me at church." Or "God took my child. Where was God when I needed him?" Maybe he has been on hold for a long while. But now is the time for you to get God back on the line in your life, because right now there may be an emergency call coming in for you.

The difference between Saul and David is clear. When David was confronted with sin, in his brokenness, he confessed, "Oh, God, I am nothing; I have sinned. You are right." He repented; he burned with shame. And God replied, "Now, David, get up and put the pieces together. Go again for me and in my name."

If you want the mind and heart of God, his will and blessing, his holiness and the best God has for your life, you must go that one way—the way of brokenness. David walked that way. Saul would not. What about you?

2
National Panic: God's Answer

1 Samuel 16:1-13

Then Samuel took the horn of oil, and anointed him in the midst of his brethren: and the Spirit of the Lord came upon David from that day forward (1 Sam. 16:13).

A NEW KING

In the life of a nation, the selection of a new leader is vastly important. This is true especially if the old leader has failed miserably in office or has stayed in power too long. A time of national panic or crisis, such as war or economic emergency, also makes a people abnormally cautious in this selection process.

King Saul failed his commission, failed Samuel, failed God. Soon everyone knew that Saul was a man's man, but not God's man. Therefore, he was not a fit ruler for God's peculiar people, the Israelites. Thus, the power of God left his reign and his life (1 Sam. 16:14). Samuel mourned and cried because he had seen in Saul's reign great promise, the promise of the nation being in the hands of a visionary, gifted man, as the people followed his leadership. Samuel cried until God dealt with his prophet. "How long will you weep over Saul? He has failed me; he has failed the people. Samuel, go and anoint a new king." Some three thousand years ago Samuel made that pilgrimage to the little town of Bethlehem, located in a tenth-class state, for the purpose of anointing *God's choice* for king.

It is difficult to imagine the excitement that was generated in

Bethlehem when the news was broadcast: "Here comes the judge." Samuel was not only a prophet but also a judge. Bethlehem was off the circuit; it was not a part of his usual rounds. Perhaps an old farmer noticed the prophet-judge coming, and he sent runners into the city to tell the mayor and the aldermen, "The judge is coming to Bethlehem, of all places." The news began to spread and people began to talk.

I can hear Abe say to Dan, "Samuel's coming! He's found out about the land you are trying to sell to the widow Haran, and he's coming to bring you into court. I told you not to try that trick." And Dan retorted, "Oh, no, don't worry about me. You worry about yourself, Abe. You're the one who sold that bull to Ben, and the bull died the next day! You should have returned his money!"

Finally, the mayor and a few aldermen had a brief city council meeting to discuss the matter. Why was Samuel coming? Was he coming as a judge or as a prophet? Was he coming for civil reasons or for religious reasons? And they rushed out to meet him and greeted him with bowing and ostentatious words of praise about his leadership and about his insight. Then in a nervous, hesitant manner they asked, "Ah, by the way, Samuel, did you come for a joyous occasion? Did you come to bring peace?" And Samuel answered, "I came to sacrifice." What a sigh of relief! "Oh, thank goodness, it's for religious reasons!"

Everybody needs a little religion. Sing a few songs or give some money; a little talk about God never hurt anybody. Religion is all right if it doesn't get down into the daily dealings of life. At this point we still have some difficulty with words such as honesty and integrity. As long as religion stays in its place, sacrifice is all right. Actually, the people in Bible times liked to sacrifice because it meant a meal of hot roast beef or lamb! Their problem, like ours, was obedience!

The Bible tells us that Samuel was driving a heifer out in front of him. He brought the meal with him. They would sing and maybe dance, pray a little, sacrifice, and eat plenty. Samuel announced, "Bring all of your family and make sure that you bring all of your sons."

Now, we do not know exactly what transpired in a service of sacrifice, but I can guess, for religion does not change much across

DAVID: AFTER GOD'S OWN HEART

the generations. I am sure that they brought the best musicians which they could muster from that little village. They wanted to make a good show for Samuel. And I almost can hear Samuel singing resoundingly in his deep bass voice—a little out of tune and flat. Jesse brought all of his sons to the feast. (Well, almost.) As Samuel greeted the people one after another, he looked for God's choice. He had one bit of information: One of Jesse's boys was to be the new king, and God would tell him which one. I imagine that Samuel drew Jesse aside and told him, "Jesse, don't mention this to anybody, but one of your sons will be the next king of Israel." What pride came to that old farmer! Something happened inside of him. "Ah, one of my boys will be the king!" Imagine it!!

PERFECTION OF THE FLESH

In time, Jesse gathered his family together and brought them to Samuel individually. "Here's my oldest son, Eliab." He wore sergeant stripes on his arm because he fought in Saul's army. Eliab was tall and strong, and he looked kind of like Saul, the king who had failed. The Bible relates that Samuel thought in his mind, *Surely this is the one.* And God told him, "He's not the one! Don't pay attention to how tall and handsome he is. Remember, I know his heart." Does it seem strange to you that Samuel almost made the same mistake again? It shouldn't, for we make the same mistakes over and over. We, too, forget that God puts little value on outward appearance.

Eliab was not the one, and so Jesse introduced Abinadab. But he was not the chosen son either. Next came Shammah. The answer was the same "no." Four more sons paraded by. There were seven sons in all. Remember, in the Bible seven is the number of perfection. I think that these sons represent the perfection of the flesh. They had every external feature you would desire in a man or in a king, but none was God's choice.

How do we make decisions about employees? Or that person for whom we will work? About our friends? Or about those people we want to know? Normally, we look at external details. In his book *Hide and Seek*, James Dobson writes that the most important asset a person in America can have is physical attractiveness. The idea begins when a baby is born. At a very early age, a little one begins to sense whether or not he is cute. That's right! How we look at the world and how the world looks at us seems to depend primarily upon our physical appearance.

Young mothers sometimes become depressed, especially after the birth of their first child. Oh, they have seen other newborn babies, but somehow when their child is born, they are expecting that four-month-old Gerber baby with teeth and hair and rosy cheeks. Then the doctor comes in and hands them a bald-headed, toothless, shriveled-up, prune-like, squealing, crying creature. "This is your baby!"

Then the baby grows and matures. At an early age that child decides how the world sees him. If the child is attractive, he grows up thinking that the world is a warm, fine place. But if the child is homely, he has the idea that the world is hard, cold, and critical. We choose people as we choose products: by the packaging. Tragic, isn't it?

The story of *The Ugly Duckling* is a good illustration of how we reinforce this idea. Here was this ugly little duck despised by all the other ducks. But the ugly duckling grew up to be a beautiful swan! What about the ugly duckling who never becomes the beautiful swan? What about *Sleeping Beauty*? Would the prince have kissed Sleeping Beauty if she had been named "Sleeping Ugly"? What about *Rudolph, the Red-nosed Reindeer*? (Oh, how he was treated because of his nose! He couldn't play in any of the reindeer games—because of his nose.) He had to perform a fabulous feat by leading Santa through a foggy, snowy night in order to be a hero, so everybody would accept him in spite of his bulbous red nose. What about *Dumbo*, the elephant with big ears? Oh, what a rough time he had until he learned how to fly!

In our culture, unless a person is handsome, intelligent, wealthy, or well-born, he is in trouble. The ugly, dumb, or poor hardly have a chance. We put inordinate pride in physical details. This fact has been true through the years. Samuel would have selected those three sons who looked so good, who stood so tall, who had all the external kingly features, but God advised Samuel, "Don't look at the outside. Look at the heart. That's how I make my choices."

"Jesse," inquired Samuel, "don't you have another boy?"

DAVID: AFTER GOD'S OWN HEART

Samuel was confused! God had declared that the new king would be one of Jesse's sons. Jesse answered, "Well, I've got my youngster" (The word "young" has about it a bad connotation in the Hebrew!). "I've got a boy who keeps the sheep." David was the eighth son of Jesse by his second wife, who had previously been married to Nabash. Jesse had seven sons and two daughters. She had brought all of her children into the family, and then together they had this eighth son, David. This child had to look up to all of his older half-brothers, who seemed to despise this misfitted little genius. David was tougher and more tenacious mentally and physically than all these big, strong, muscular older brothers. He played musical instruments, sang, and looked at the heavens. "We're sort of ashamed of little brother," Jesse implied.

"Bring him," commanded Samuel. When David walked in, I think that every eye turned. He was a contrast. He looked different with his auburn hair and (maybe) his steely blue eyes. Samuel walked over to him and anointed him with that little horn of oil. Josephus, the historian, wrote that Samuel whispered to the shepherd boy, "You will be the next king." And nobody knew his name!

THE HEART OF DAVID

God saw qualities in that shepherd which his father and mother, his brethren, and his neighbors did not see. This boy was not highly prized—an outcast and a nobody was a king! Paul wrote to the church at Corinth:

> 27 But God hath chosen the foolish things of the world to confound the wise; and God hath chosen the weak things of the world to confound the things which are mighty; 28 And base things of the world, and things which are despised, hath God chosen, yea. And things which are not, to bring to naught things that are: 29 That no flesh should glory in his presence (1 Cor. 1:27-29).

God's choices are different from ours so we cannot boast! When we think we are something—that we have gifts, talents, or abilities, or that our appearance, mental prowess, family connection, or wealth is important, then we boast: "You know, I had a part in that. Look what I did." But if we are base and weak and foolish nobodies and do that which is honored by the Lord, we have to confess, "Oh, God, I had nothing to do with it! All I am, all I have is because of you." God gets the glory!

Man looks at the outside; God looks at the heart. What kind of heart did he see in David? He saw the young heart which wrote the shepherd's psalm, Psalm 23.

1 *"The Lord is my shepherd; I shall not want."* He saw a believing heart. 2 *"He maketh me to lie down in green pastures: he leadeth me beside the still waters.* 3 *He restoreth my soul:"* He saw a meditating heart. *"He leadeth me in the paths of righteousness for his name's sake."* He saw a holy heart set on the right path.

4 *"Yea, though I walk through the valley of the shadow of death, I will fear no evil: for thou art with me, thy rod and thy staff they comfort me."* He saw a courageous heart. 5 *"Thou preparest a table before me in the presence of mine enemies: thou anointest my head with oil; my cup runneth over."* He saw a thankful heart. 6 *"Surely goodness and mercy shall follow me all the days of my life: and I will dwell in the house of the Lord forever."* He saw a heart fixed on God. *"My heart is fixed, O God, my heart is fixed"* (Ps. 57:7).

THE GIANT OF PREPARATION

How did David develop these characteristics? He was unwanted and abused, from a broken family, pushed to the backside of those Judean hills to look after mangy, stinking sheep. How did God build this heart? What school did he attend? He attended God's school! Alexander Maclaren observed that he attended the school of *solitude*. David sang the psalms, prayed the prayers, tended the sheep, while he was thinking those thoughts of God in the school of solitude. How important it is that we let nature speak to us alone. Strength of character is built in times of meditative solitude.

Also, David learned away from the public eye. After he was anointed by Samuel, what did he do? He went back to tend the sheep. How do we know this? When Saul wanted David to play for him, he was with the sheep (1 Sam. 16:19). When Jesse sent food to the front lines, where the soldiers were fighting prior to

DAVID: AFTER GOD'S OWN HEART

David's battle with Goliath, what was he doing? He was tending the sheep (1 Sam. 17:15 *ff.*). David did the menial tasks first in solitude and obscurity. Most of us want to do the sensational. We want to stand up front; we want to be in charge. But David was faithful, though unnoticed.

As God looks on the hearts of people today, he sees a mother washing dishes, cooking meals, running carpools, sorting clothes, caring for children: nothing glamorous about that, but God honors the commitment, nevertheless. The office worker going over stacks of papers and working out countless details is often seen by God alone. The Sunday School teacher who spends the week studying the Bible and asking God for his Word to that class is rewarded in countless ways. We pray and study in obscurity and solitude for the moments when God touches us and calls us to do something for him; then we are prepared. We have a reservoir of strength when we have "soaked" with the Lord alone. When we have been faithful in the little things, and when God says, "Come up higher," it is because he prepared us in solitude. God is making ready leaders for tomorrow in quiet, unseen, unexpected places. These people are not pushing and promoting themselves; they are growing in the wisdom of God.

David was prepared through labor. His work as a shepherd was real! When he saw a lion, he attacked and killed the beast. Evidently, he killed a bear with his hands (1 Sam. 17:34-36). Want to try that? He was not simply enjoying a mystical monastic existence. There was flesh and blood and reality in defending and caring for the sheep. God was preparing a young man's heart for signal service and witness. Character cannot be built otherwise. And God is never in a hurry to build his way, his heart, and his character in a man or woman.

KNOWING GOD

God had been preparing David in his "Judean School of the Wilderness" for many years. However, the pivotal point about David is not so much that he knew God, but that *God knew him.* The most salient fact for any person is that God knows him. People who really know God have boundless energy for God; they have boldness for him. They have a sense of God about their lives, their words, and their walk.

The more complex something is, the more difficult it is to know and understand. We can know a language, a building, or even the Smithsonian, but when we know a person, we have accomplished a more difficult feat. When a man comments, "I know that horse," he probably means he has ridden the horse, handled the horse. He knows the nature and character of the horse. However, if I say, "I know that man" or "I know that woman," I am speaking of tremendous complexity in a human being. Maybe a person can know almost everything he needs to know about a horse in a week or two—perhaps less; but a person can "know" another for months, for years, for decades, and not *really know* them. The more complex and complicated, the more involved, the more agendas the person has, the more difficult he is to know. For someone to testify, "I know God," is to say, "I know this Being, this eternal Being. He is perfect; he is all-powerful; he is all-knowing. He is the Creator, the Sustainer. I *know* God!" Think about it! God in all of his omnipotence and omniscience has to desire to know us continually, if we are really to know him.

In his epic novel *The Winds of War*, Herman Wouk tells the story of Commander Pug Henry, a navy man who was assigned to one desk job after another during the beginning years of World War II, when his heart yearned for a battleship. Although the probability of a man of his rank doing so is slight, he conferred with all the heads of state, at one time or another, as the drama unfolded. Pug's first encounter with President Roosevelt came as a surprise. All he had been told was what to wear and when he would be picked up. On numerous occasions thereafter, he was called to visit with the president concerning the progress of the war. Together with their families, they dined at the White House. They were on trains and ships and talked at all hours of the day and night. They discussed Lend Lease, the Atlantic Charter, and various developments and agreements. And they became good friends—at the president's instigation.

If the president of the United States invited me to the White House for a visit, regardless of my party preference, I would find time to go. Then suppose that when I met him, he treated me in a perfunctory, professional manner, was nice and cordial, and sent me on my way. But what if he drew me to one side? Suppose he

DAVID: AFTER GOD'S OWN HEART

really listened to me, and when I left he insisted, "We need to talk again"? The next time we visited we had a meal together. Then, over a period of time, I became a friend with the president of the United States of America. What an overwhelming responsibility such a relationship would carry because of his office and because of who he is. How well I know the president depends upon how well he wants me to know him. Maybe I want to know him and to spend time with him. I want us to work together; I want to advise him and travel with him. Oh, no! This relationship would come only at his initiative because he is the president!

How well do you want to know God? Because God is God, the major part of the friendship is at his invitation. Therefore, we ask, "God, how much do you want to know me?" And God says, "Oh, I want to know you so much that I sent my Son down to show you what I'm like. In fact, he died just for you. I want to know you so much that your name is in the scars of his hands. I want to know you so much that every moment of every day, your name is on my lips. Through every step you take, every thought you have, my mind is right with you, loving you and caring for you. I want to cleanse everything in your life so you'll be able to walk and talk with me."

The symbolism in the Bible of the relationship of the Son of God to God is like that of the sheep to the shepherd. It is like the son is to the father or the wife is to the husband. God wants to know us so much that he keeps on reaching and touching, convincing, forgiving, and healing. He does whatever is necessary to reach through to us, because he wants to know us so much. We never have to worry about God discovering something about us which he doesn't already know. He cannot find any evil or immoral thought or action which will surprise him. Isn't that something? God knows you and he knows me, and he doesn't look on the outside! He looks at our hearts, our motivations. He knows what we really are.

And one other point: We know God just as much as *we want* to know him. God wants to give us all of himself. He keeps loving, caring, forgiving, cleansing. It is wonderful to know God, but it is even more wonderful to know that he knows us!

The answer to national panic is leadership that calls the Almighty by his first name—Jesus!

3
The Mismatch

1 Samuel 17:4-8

And David said to Saul, Let no man's heart fail because of him; thy servant will go and fight with this Philistine (1 Sam. 17:32).

The "apple" is the center of the eyeball. In Old Testament days, when someone said, "I am going to hurt you seriously," usually he tried to put out the eye of his enemy. He tried to scar the "apple." Before the days of protective lenses or even contact lenses, or ophthalmology, when a person's eye was injured, many times he would become blind. The word "David" means "the apple of God's eye." David, a man after the heart of God—biblically speaking—was special to God. He was the apple of God's eye.

I sort of believe he had an I.Q. of 150-plus. David had military genius which may never have been duplicated in subsequent history. He led a weak nation to a posture of strength. David enjoyed unusual athletic skills and all the acumen which one could desire. Combine those innate gifts with God's special blessing and you had a phenomenal individual. *Question:* Why is the biography of David in the Scriptures? Perhaps it is there to make us feel inferior! No! The story of David is in the Bible to teach us that when we live God's way, there is victory and success, but when we live a life-style of the flesh, there is always failure, frustration, and disaster. This was even true of a king who seemed to have every human base covered.

David was anointed, but his life-style did not change very much.

He kept tending the sheep, but God was preparing David for things to come! So many times I look back across my years and consider events that happened when I was a child or a teenager in school. I remember how I spent my time and studies; and I question, "How in the world is this ever going to help me?" But I'm always amazed that in time, something would happen and I'd have some insight or some knowledge, and I'd say, "You know, I never thought that would be of any use to me." How God prepares us through crisis, through blessing, through opportunity! He puts us exactly where he wants us to be, with all the resources and abilities necessary to do his task.

While David was in the wilderness, alone with the sheep, he became a dreamer. He looked at the stars and the sun and the mountains; he learned how to dream. He had visions and expansive thoughts about God. David learned how to sing and how to play the harp. He composed psalms. He fell in love with the sheep. The child who does not have love and acceptance at home will give his affection to a pet. This is what David did. He loved those sheep. This fact is clearly evident in the Psalms. However, I think David primarily came to know God. The Lord was preparing him in the quiet places for the public ministry which was to follow. Also, David became a fighter. At home, he was an outcast, ridiculed by his family and sent away at a young age to work at a thankless, lonely task. He could have surrendered to his circumstances as he became withdrawn and dull. But he was a fighter, a survivor.

He had spent years tending the sheep and developing his heart and mind. During those obscure years, David grew in his knowledge of God. Ideas, dreams, visions, and musical talent stretched his capacity. A tenacious determination, coupled with a disciplined life, produced a man who learned how to win. This was the shepherd boy, David.

A battle was underway with the Philistines, a strong nation, with the best-equipped army on the face of the earth. They had almost exclusive rights to all the iron, the number-one metal. These warlike people were well-trained and experienced; they had vast supplies of armor—helmets, shields, swords, and spears. The Hebrews were farmers, hill people. They were agricultural people, not fighters. The Philistines more or less tolerated them. They would collect taxes and exploit them periodically, but as long as the Hebrews stayed in the mountains, the Philistines co-existed in the fertile valleys.

Without warning, there was trouble in the area of the tribe of Benjamin, and Saul went out, along with Abner, his commander-in-chief, and their volunteer army, to defend their interests in the hill country. David's older brothers, Sergeant Eliab, Corporal Abinadab, and Private Shammah were in the army. In the middle of the military impasse, Jesse told David, "We must take supplies to Saul's army." Jesse gave David ten loaves of bread and a sack of grain. And he said, "Here, I want you to take ten cheeses along and give them to the officers, and make sure you tell them this came from Eliab's father. I want that boy to get a commission one of these days. Now, David, don't get into any trouble. We know your crazy ways! You might do anything. You just do what I tell you. Stay out of the way. You're still a shepherd boy."

With those instructions, David went to the front lines. Oh, how excited he was! I cannot imagine what he expected. He already had fought more battles in his mind than the world would ever envision. He was surprised by what he found. He saw the Philistine army at the edge of the valley, the Hebrews in the hill country, and no one could move. The Philistines could not defeat the Hebrews, for the Hebrews had the higher, rocky ground. The Hebrews had only spears and rocks for weapons, but the Philistines could not climb up with all their armor. Also, Saul's army had gravity on their side. In short, if the Philistines tried to advance, they would be slaughtered. If the Hebrews went down into the valley, on level ground, they did not have a chance. The area was so mountainous that the Philistines could not encircle the Hebrews. Furthermore, a little brook separated the forces. David realized that they had been in that situation for many days, and he commented, "Boy, this is the way you fight, huh? Just sit around and talk, play cards, shoot dice, complain, dream of going back home. Is this it?" But then he heard some of the soldiers talking. "I sure hope he doesn't come back this afternoon."

David inquired, "Who are you talking about?" They asked, "Son, where have you been? Did you just get here? Why, the

DAVID: AFTER GOD'S OWN HEART

Philistines have the biggest guy you've ever seen! Abner our CO says he's under ten feet tall; but when he puts that big brass helmet on, he looks like he's twelve feet tall! He's got a coat of mail, boots, shin guards, and shoulder guards incorporating over two hundred pounds of equipment. He has a spear that's made out of brass with a fifteen-pound head on it. He marches out once or twice a day and when the sun hits all that brass, I'll tell you, son, it's something to see! It's frightening! Abner and Saul get out of the way, and act like they're making big plans and that they don't hear him. He marches up and down, cursing and challenging God and intimidating all of Israel."

David answered, "I sure would like to see that fellow!" And the soldiers remarked, "Listen, you don't want to see him! But if you are serious, be here the first thing in the morning."

I imagine that David reported to Jesse, "We need a little more food there at the front lines. The boys are having a rough time. Going to be there for awhile. Nobody can make a move." Early the next morning, David was down on the front row waiting for the Goliath show. As the sun rose, Goliath marched out; he taunted the soldiers and shouted obscenities. For over forty days, usually twice a day, he had been coming closer and closer to the troops.

David looked at him. He said, "Hmm, that big galoot is just waiting to get clobbered! I can take him!" Some of the soldiers laughed, "Sure you can, son. Oh, we're confident you can. Go get him! Did you hear what the shepherd boy said? He said he could take him!" David defended himself, "I can kill that guy. He's profaning God. God's on our side!"

"Sure God is, son. That's right. God's on our side. But look at Goliath!"

About this time, Eliab, David's brother with all the stripes, walked up. "Little brother, what are you doing down here? This isn't a show; this is *war*, boy! You go back to your sheep and get out of the way. You're always causing trouble!" David said, "What did I do? Isn't there a cause?" David just walked away and continued talking to the other soldiers. "I can take that guy. I can take him!" Abner must have heard about it, because he took David to Saul. Since David was the first volunteer, they listened to

THE MISMATCH

him. "You know, I can handle him." And Saul replied, "Go back to your sheep. I appreciate your bravery, but you're just a kid."

But there was something about David! There was a gleam in his eye; God was in his life. His spirit was contagious. Suddenly David countered, "I killed the lion and the bear, and I can handle that heathen." Saul must have remembered something about the Spirit of God which he once had. He replied, "Well, go ahead. But if you must fight, I want you to use my armor and my sword." And David put on Saul's armor, but it was not his style. He had no idea how to use all of that gear. It didn't fit. "I can't fight like that; I've got to do it my way." He took off the armor and went out.

Goliath had paraded around almost long enough. He really enjoyed these daily displays of power, but he was becoming hot in all that armor under the sweltering sun. Out of the corner of his eye he must have seen David coming. "Look at that dumb kid. Reckon he doesn't know I'm here? He's going to get hurt. These shepherd kids don't have any sense." And he must have taken his spear and struck a rock to get David's attention. "Get out of here. I'm going to feed you to the birds! This is war; you're going to get killed! Go on back to your sheep."

Then David preached a little sermon, but what a sermon! He preached in the name of God, and Goliath was infuriated. He roared, "Am I a dog? Here you come with a stick and a sling!" He began to curse David (Have you noticed that the people who don't have the mental ability or the vocabulary often resort to profanity?). David moved in about the distance that a pitcher would be from the catcher. The Bible states that he reached down into the little brook and selected five smooth stones. Now, those five stones tell us something of the secret David had in his life which only God could see.

He had prepared for this encounter with Goliath for years. That sling and those stones made a deadly weapon in the hands of one who had practiced with all sorts of targets in the hills. He had used his man-powered "gun" to discourage attacks on his sheep by wild animals. In his spare time, he probably had felled numerous imaginary giants. David was ready; his aim was accurate.

But David picked up five stones; he needed only one! Maybe his computer-like mind immediately organized alternative offensives. He had ability. But notice the one quality of life which made him a real champion: humility. Without the Lord, he could have been a skilled warrior, but the way in which David depended upon God strengthened his character and increased his effectiveness. He thought, "I'm a champion, but without God, that's all I am."

In a moment, the first stone whizzed through the air. Dead center! The middle of the frontal bone! Down went Goliath with his armor crashing on the rocks and echoing all through the valley of Elah. Quicker than a flash of lightning, David took Goliath's own sword and cut off his head. It was all over. Then Abner and Saul, sensing victory, gave the battle cry. Suddenly, the Hebrews were brave. They came swarming down from the hill country with their rocks and spears flying. The Philistines could not believe it! They ran for their lives and left their weaponry behind for the victorious farmers to use against them!

HOW TO FIGHT GIANTS

When we read between the lines of 1 Samuel 17, we learn some biblical principles we need to know as we encounter the giants in our lives. We wrestle giants all the time! How we need help!

Principle Number One: We prepare to fight giants in secret places. Battles are won in closets, in wildernesses, in obscure places. We become the persons which we are when we are alone! We cannot wait until the moment of decision—the moment of contest, the moment of temptation, the moment of adversity, the moment when the bad report comes in from the pathologist—to battle these giants. David was ready for that public encounter, because in private, through those years, he knew God.

Principle Number Two: Giants keep coming. Just as Goliath came day after day, twice a day, so giants keep coming. When we have battled a giant, another one comes. Often, a giant returns for a rematch. The battleground for a Christian is a process of growth in Jesus Christ. We never arrive on higher ground where we can settle back and enjoy life with no giants! Ah, the giants keep coming.

Principle Number Three: Know a giant when you see one. If Eliab had asked us, as he did David, "What are you doing here on the front line? Go back home and look after the sheep. Who do you think you are, you smart-aleck kid," we would have fought Eliab! But he was not the giant—Goliath was. You see, we Christians fight among ourselves. Denominations and groups battle one another all the time. Within churches, we fight for position, for rank, for prestige, when we should be fighting the heathen giants, the pagan strongholds of satanic influence.

Principle Number Four: Do not listen to carnal advice. Saul represents a person who follows God in a carnal way. He said, "David, you're too small. You must fight the way I fight. Use my armor, my sword." He was looking on the external appearance. When we go out to do spiritual battle, and we use the world's wisdom, we will lose every time. David knew that he had to go out in the armor of God. Ephesians 6:11 speaks of "the whole armor of God." How often "Saul's armor" seems best! We fight people with their own weapons, and we lose because the warfare is a spiritual one.

Principle Number Five: Fighting giants often is an intimidating experience. Giants threaten us. We encounter problems and difficulties, and we are frightened and inhibited. David was not intimidated, because in his heart he knew that, *"If God be for us, who can be against us?"* (Rom. 8:31). Because God saw that Goliath was a mismatch, God was on David's side. Goliath didn't have a chance! David refused to be bullied or overwhelmed; he was in control because God was controlling him.

Principle Number Six: Giant-fighting is a lonely experience. David went down into that valley alone. When giants come, we can get counsel and help, but ultimately we have to go out and handle the problem alone.

Principle Number Seven: Know what to remember. David said, "I fought a lion and a bear, and I defeated them." Do you know what the problem is with many of us? We remember what we need to forget, and we forget what we need to remember! We tend to recall only the bad experiences. "I had surgery back there." "Let me tell you, I just struck out." "I'm the world's worst." "I went bankrupt one time; I couldn't pay my bills." The devil would keep us defeated all the time! We need to remember our victories. After killing Goliath, David took the sword and all the paraphernalia of

34   **DAVID: AFTER GOD'S OWN HEART**

Goliath, and the Bible reports that he put them in his tent. They were his trophies!

Have you ever received a trophy? If you have, I guarantee that you didn't throw it away! We put our trophies in prominent places. Also, we need to keep our spiritual trophies. David put the sword of Goliath in the house of God. Years later when he needed a sword, he used it again in battle. When we defeat a giant, to keep that trophy in our minds and hearts, we need to use that victory to help us defeat another giant.

Our equipment for fighting giants is the same David had: the stone of humility and the sling of faith. We can conquer all the giants in the world because the Lord Jesus Christ is in our lives. He has prepared us for battle in those secret places. We can say, "Hey. Come on, giants! Because if you take me on, it's a mismatch! God has equipped me to do battle with all the giants who come my way." Are you equipped like that?

4
The Toughest Challenge: Success

1 Samuel 17:55—18:12

Saul hath slain his thousands, and David his ten thousands (1 Sam. 18:7).

Nobody dreamed that David would kill the giant Goliath. This young lad who was less than twenty years of age, under six feet tall, who had never worn an "Israeli" army uniform, never had a sword in his hand, never had fought in a single military battle in his life, never had marched even one time in the armies of Saul. Think about it—he was willing to fight in hand-to-hand combat the undisputed, heavyweight, martial-arts, military champion of the world, Goliath. With a swoosh of David's sling, Goliath was dead. Are you ready for that even after all these thousands of years? Was David ready for it when it happened that day? The result for David was instant fame, popularity, and prosperity. He could handle Goliath, but could he handle success?

Thomas Carlisle opined, "For every one person who can stand up under success, there are a hundred persons who can stand up under adversity." It is much easier to fail! Tom Landry commented that coaching is more difficult when the team wins. "I know what to do when we lose. I can instruct them; I can get them up; I can show them where they've made mistakes; I can challenge them; I can talk about their sitting on the bench, or having a contract cut, or not renewing it the next year. But," he said, "when we win—

that's the challenge of coaching. It is exceedingly difficult to be a winner and to coach a winning team."

Elvis Presley, the highest-paid performer in the history of this world, never came to terms with his own success and popularity. John Lucas, the number-one draft pick in the NBA for the Rockets, is a good illustration of what happens to so many young athletes. They step out of college, or they leave college early, and suddenly they are millionaires with national fame and prominence. There is a hit movie with a Marilyn Monroe or a hit television series with a Freddie Prinz. What happens? Or there is a young couple on a ranch trying to scratch out a meager existence with a few cows, and "black gold" begins to erupt from the bottom of that little ranch. Overnight they are multimillionaires. What happens? In the history of the Bible and of mankind, rapid success and prosperity usually breed mediocrity, and many times breed tragedy. "Too much, too soon" is the story of many a life. Take a long look at David because he knew how to succeed. In his life there are beautiful principles that will hold us in good stead when we make it, get it, or find it. The severest challenge of any life is how to deal with prosperity and success.

A friend of mine gave his son a little go-cart—much to my dismay (I have seen and presided over too many tragedies across these years which resulted from such motor vehicles.). The boy would drive that go-cart into the ground, around and around a little dirt track, and then he would go to his dad and beg, "Dad, fix it." And his dad would get out the manual, find what to do, and try to fix it. One day his father, being a fine Christian, decided that he would use the manual as an illustration to his boy. "What does this manual teach us?" the father asked.

The son, about eleven years old, said, "Well, it tells us what to do when the go-cart won't work." The father continued, "Well, what else is in this manual?" "It tells you how to maintain the go-cart so it won't get in trouble."

"That's right, Son." Then he gave his son a little lecture about maintaining the go-cart and decided to apply the lesson to a bigger realm: the father added, "Do you think God is smarter than the manufacturers of that go-cart?" The boy thought, "Here comes the sermon," but he answered, "Yes, I think God is smarter."

THE TOUGHEST CHALLENGE: SUCCESS   **37**

"Well, did God make us?" "Yes, Dad, God made us."

"Wonderful, wonderful. Do you think he gave us an instruction book?" "Yes, Dad, I know about the Bible."

"What does the Bible do?" "Well, it tells us how to fix things when they get broken and it tells us how to maintain things so they won't get broken."

Is that too simple? I think not. Consider success from the biblical point of view. As we build into our lives principles for living with success, we find that this is indeed the greatest challenge any person will ever have!

RELATIONSHIP—SUBMISSION

We must understand David's interpersonal relationships: how he got along with people after fame and stardom. In his dealings with King Saul, David was submissive. Four times in 1 Samuel 18, we read that David conducted himself "wisely" (vv. 5,14,15,30). All the servants of Saul admired David, and he was made commander-in-chief of the men of war (v. 5). Even the old, hardened soldiers recognized integrity in this young man who slew the giant. He was fair and even-handed with privates and generals. David conducted himself wisely and was submissive to King Saul.

Through the years, I have interviewed many people for church staff positions. Some of those folks have had all the credentials: an impressive dossier which described extensive education, a well-formed biographical sketch, and awesome references. But if the applicant began to criticize or complain about their present employer, I checked them off without exception! The person might seem to be fitted for the task, but if he were disloyal to his supervisor in one situation, he would normally be as disloyal in another.

Work for that person who pays your check! Be loyal; praise your bosses; make them a success—no matter how unworthy they are! This is God's chain of command. Many problems at work are caused by Christians who whine, complain, and undercut with the language of Zion! They are discredited in the business world because they are not loyal; they are not submissive. If your supervisor tells you to do something, do it to the best of your ability and let him/her have the credit! God will honor your effort and attitude.

David was submissive to Saul; he was loyal. He played the harp for him, praised him, and fought in battles for him. David gave Saul the credit.

RELATIONSHIP—FRIENDSHIP

Look at David's friendship with Jonathan. This was the most telling relationship. David's friendship with Jonathan tells us more about his character than any of his other relationships. As long as Jonathan was alive, David had a friend. David walked with God; he was a man above reproach. David was a man after God's own heart. After Jonathan was killed in battle, David's life was never the same. After David had killed Goliath, David and Saul talked. "And it came to pass, when he had made an end of speaking unto Saul, that the soul of Jonathan was knit with the soul of David, and Jonathan loved him as his own soul" (1 Sam. 18:1). Their souls were knit together. There was immediate rapport and they became friends.

Jonathan had a right to the throne by virtue of his birth; David had a claim to the throne by virtue of the anointing of Samuel. These two should have been clashing with one another! But their souls were knit together. They said, "We will stick together and not let the throne stand in our way." And Jonathan humbled himself and said, "David, when you're on the throne, I will serve you at your right hand, and we'll set this nation on its feet." Jonathan was a great man.

Jonathan reached down to this shepherd boy, David. To understand this situation, suppose you are a British war hero. After you return home, you are touring Buckingham Palace. Suddenly the entire royal family appears, dressed in their royal robes. You whisper to the tour guide, "This is some tour!" You try to reach for your camera when Prince Charles steps forward and calls your name, "Would you come before us?" With fear and trembling, you bow down before royalty. Then Prince Charles comes up to you, removes his royal robe, and puts it on you. He puts his scepter in your right hand; he puts his signet ring on your finger; then he puts a crown on your head. Everyone exclaims, "Look! The hero has become royalty! He's in the ruling class."

That is what happened to David; that is what Jonathan did for David. Jonathan gave David his robe and other garments, as well as his sword and his bow. And I am sure that David tried to reciprocate! Maybe he gave Jonathan his prize sheep! They became intimate friends. Literally, they became blood brothers; theirs was a covenant relationship.

The Hebrew tradition of the blood covenant was an intricate ceremony which marked the beginning of an irrevocable relationship. First Samuel 18:1-4, as well as the remainder of the story of David and Jonathan, indicates that they had entered into such a covenant; they were blood brothers.

> 1 *And it came to pass, when he had made an end of speaking unto Saul, that the soul of Jonathan was knit with the soul of David, and Jonathan loved him as his own soul. 2 And Saul took him that day, and would let him go no more home to his father's house. 3 Then Jonathan and David made a covenant, because he loved him as his own soul. 4 And Jonathan stripped himself of the robe that was upon him, and gave it to David, and his garments, even to his sword, and to his bow, and to his girdle.*

In the first part of the blood covenant ceremony, the two men would exchange coats or "robes." The outer garment was a symbol of warmth and also indicated family identity. Then they gave each other their weapons: sword, shield, bow. Thus, they promised to defend each other against all enemies.

Sacrifice was involved next. Then they took an animal and cut it in half and spread it open. Then the men stood back to back and walked through the blood between the halves of the animal in a figure 8. Then each man cut his own wrist, and then they held their arms above their heads, with the blood streaming down their arms. They tied their wrists so that their blood flowed together. A handshake followed, with the blood between their hands, indicating the giving of themselves to each other. Afterwards, they put powder into the wounds so a scar would always remain as evidence of this relationship.

Each man took on the name of the other and gave his blood brother all of his belongings. In the final part of the ceremony, the

40   DAVID: AFTER GOD'S OWN HEART

men ate a meal together. They broke the bread and gave it to each other, saying, "This is my body; I am a part of you." Then they drank the cup together and promised, "This is my blood. I am in you, and you are in me."

Proverbs contains a little verse which hints of this blood brother relationship and so accurately describes David's friendship with Jonathan: *. . . and there is a friend that sticketh closer than a brother* (Prov. 18:24).

But Jonathan also remained loyal to Saul, even when Saul turned in a jealous rage on David. Many times Jonathan would reprimand Saul and try to make him understand that David was on his side; David was fighting for him. He was loyal to the king. But Saul did not understand. *Greater love hath no man than this, that a man lay down his life for his friends* (John 15:13). The Bible says that Jonathan loved David "as his own soul" (1 Sam. 18:3). Jonathan was able to maintain his covenant relationship with David, as well as loyalty to his father; he went to his death at his father's side. A person is indeed fortunate who has one, two, or three intimate friends. It is important for everybody to have friends. Anyone who does not have a genuine, intimate friend is missing out in life. Even Jesus, our own Savior and Lord, had his friends, his apostles, his intimates.

What are some of the characteristics of true friendship which we identify in the relationship between Jonathan and David? First we see that genuine friendship is generous. Jonathan gave to David— David gave to Jonathan. There was a sense of spontaneous generosity between them. Special friends help us learn what Jesus meant when he said, *It is more blessed to give than to receive* (Acts 20:35). We want God's best for an intimate friend. Also, we don't "keep score"—we cannot do enough for a real friend.

A true friend is faithful, faithful when you are there, but more important, faithful when no one is around. A true friend is militantly loyal and faithful at all costs. In any situation he declares, "Hey, that's my friend. He's special; he's something." The principle behind the Golden Rule is "What you need is what you give": the concept of reciprocity. If you need someone to listen to—first of all you listen to somebody. If you need love—give love. If you need a friend—be a friend. Jonathan is a fitting personification of friendship. Also, with an intimate friend, you can be yourself. Say whatever you want—moan, cry—anything! Incidentally, intimate friends rarely "preach" to each other. I do not want an intimate friend who preaches to me, do you? Give a friend time to work out his difficult situations. If a friend wants counsel, he will ask for it. You will sense it. A real friend has the gift of encouragement! He will build you up when you feel down and out. He will give you a positive word, a healing word. He will praise you and will promote your cause.

SUFFERING AND PARADES

God was building David's life. God can never use a person phenomenally unless first of all that person has suffered, unless he has been deprived, unless he has gone through many trying circumstances. Instant stardom came to David, and suddenly his best friend was the prince. The submissive spirit which had been evident throughout David's life continued to be evident in his relationship with Saul. David became a part of the king's household. He was a hero to the whole nation of Israel. His song went to the top of the charts. When David came in following a victory in battle, there would be a spontaneous parade.

In my hometown at the end of World War II, pandemonium broke out when it was announced that peace had come. There was a parade with people, music, old cars. People stood on tops of buildings. We were shouting and moving up the streets, shaking hands and hugging one another! What a celebration: the Allies had won! Such was the scene in Israel when David returned from battle. Cymbals and musical instruments were resounding. There was a parade. All Israel began to dance and sing.

Once when I was in the Holy Land at the Mt. Carmel Hotel, our group was entertained with an Israeli folk dance. Merely watching the show was an exhausting experience! They moved around; they jumped; they circled one way, then another. In one number, they picked people from the audience to come and dance with them and—you guessed it—one of them picked me! Why, I was almost killed out there with those Israeli folk dancers! Now I understand what the Bible means when it refers to dancing! It was a celebration with shouting, clapping, spinning, and kicking. And David joined in the revelry.

When Saul heard that number-one hit record, he couldn't take it! He saw David: prosperous, successful, blessed, top of the heap. He was at the top of every list, hero of every boy, and the idol of every girl. The victories and parades angered Saul. Saul heard that hit tune one too many times and he thought, *I'm going to bring him down.* Saul could not live with the idea that David was more popular than he. In spite of counsel from Jonathan, Abner, and his men, Saul became increasingly determined to kill David. *"And Saul eyed David from that day and forward"* (1 Sam. 18:9).

Jealousy is a damning attitude. It makes us do terrible things. Now we are seldom jealous of the president of the United States. No competition! We are never jealous of a person who has a lower rank than ours. No competition! Jealousy comes between peers. When David reached equal acclaim with Saul, Saul could not cope. He spent the remainder of his years trying to kill David.

David had a problem: he had to kill Saul or run away. Saul had as much chance against David as Goliath did! This was a mismatch in David's favor. The Bible gives us the account of ten years in which David ran as an outcast, an outlaw, a renegade. Anyone who associated with David or helped him was under the king's condemnation of death. Where was God all these years? Did David tell God to wait while he ran from the king? Although we do not see much outward evidence of God during this period, God was actively making something out of David—in adversity! David's problem was not the temptation to kill Saul. He had plenty of occasions to do that. His problem was that of keeping himself from a position in which he would have to kill Saul. So he had to run, run, run—for ten years—until Saul was killed.

Then David became king of Judah. He had his first children in Hebron, the capital city. For seven-and-a-half years he ruled over Judah. Then he was also made king of Israel and moved the seat of government to Jerusalem. What an experience.

The Bible tells us that David and the Israelites dominated the land all the way from the sands of Egypt to the waters of the Tigris and Euphrates, often called "The Cradle of Civilization." In other words, they subdued all the people and David was king of all the land from Dan to Beersheba and beyond. How did all that happen? Surely there is a tremendous movie plot in the biblical account of how David subdued the Philistines who were far more powerful, better trained, and better equipped than Israel. However, when we look closely, we find only one little reference. *When you hear a sound like marching feet in the tops of the balsam trees, attack! For it will signify that the Lord has prepared the way for you and will destroy them* (2 Sam. 5:24, TLB). What is that? *When you hear the sound of marching feet in the balsam trees, attack!* That is the full battle account! With that, David took over the whole land.

The most exciting part of Hebrew history is not recorded! What does that mean? Succinctly, this: life is not understood by studying history alone. Life cannot be interpreted by reading the newspaper accounts of births, deaths, and marriages. The great fact in any life is not the job that person is doing for God, but the job God is doing in that person!!

David had a friend, Jonathan; and he had a friend in God. He handled success by having a friend who stood by him, who encouraged him, who protected him. He had a friend. More than that, David had a heart for God. He knew how to handle success with humility. He recognized that God's question to him, was, "David, how are you . . . inside?" And he asks that same question of you—and me.

5
When There's Nothing Left to Lean On

1 Samuel 19:10,12,18; 21:15—22:1

Surely God spares the heroes and heroines in Scripture and sets them up as models so we can see their lofty living and be drawn to them. No! The Bible never flatters its heroes. That is not how the inspired Word records the facts. The Scripture speaks a clear, understandable word; it uncovers the life of a person so we see every facet of it. Even David—the man after God's own heart—was not exempt from the analyzing gaze of the Holy Spirit. All of his sins—hypocrisy, chicanery, and lying—were not glossed over lightly.

David the super hero, David the giant killer, David the armor-bearer of Saul, David, Saul's own personal musician—this same David had all the props knocked out from under him! So many times, God positions us so we have nothing to lean on except the Almighty himself.

All of us are more "leaners" than we are "learners." We are "leaners" in the sense that we lean on a wife or a husband, or we lean on our children or our grandchildren. We lean on our appearance or we lean on our vocation or we lean on our reputation. Some lean on a special talent.

A body builder pumps iron and does strenuous exercises. What sets him apart from others is his physical strength and his appearance. It gives him recognition and identity. He leans on that aspect of his life.

God wants to take everybody on the face of this earth and place them into a position so they have absolutely nothing to lean on except him.

When you were born, basically you were alone. Oh, there was the doctor and perhaps a couple of nurses and, of course, your mother and perhaps your father. But in a sense—alone. As you grow older and your life develops, you encounter new friends and your responsibilities increase. Somewhere toward middle age, most people have a pretty broad spectrum of life. Life has dimension. Then the children leave home and as the years go by they visit less frequently. As you begin to slow down and move toward retirement, you wake up one day and discover that you are "on the shelf," and that most of life has passed by. Your realm of friendship tends to narrow. Before long many of your peers begin to die. If you live past eighty, most of your friends will have died. In your last days you will probably go into a hospital. Family and friends will come to your bedside. Then a sign will be placed on the hospital room door which reads "Family Only." Later another sign goes up: "Immediate Family Only." Life's vital signs grow weak. As you decline, you are placed in Intensive Care, where only one member of the family can visit at a time. Finally you die just as you were born—alone with God. All of life moves from the simple to the complex, and then to the simple again.

So the challenge before us is to know God and to understand that, "All other ground is sinking sand." We lean on things, we lean on people, but God wants us to lean on him alone! When we were born, we cried. Everybody else laughed and rejoiced. May we so live that when we die we will laugh and rejoice, and other people will cry. If we lean solely on Jesus Christ, that kind of life can be ours.

David had many props early in life, but as quick as a flash, God began to pull those props out from under him. In a few months David began to lose everything he had been leaning on.

WHAT A WIFE!

When David first had to flee from Saul, he ran home. He ran home to Michal. Michal was Saul's daughter. When Saul gave her to David he said, "I will give him her that she may be a snare to him" (1 Sam. 18:21). Saul thought, *If I can get David to marry*

Michal, my problems will be over. She is so much trouble; she has so many agendas going; she will take care of any possibility of David succeeding at anything. How many times women like Michal have destroyed the potentiality in a man!

When David ran to Michal, she appeared to be a loyal wife. Michal said, "You'd better flee out of the window by night" (cf. 1 Sam. 19:12 *ff.*). Michal helped him escape through the window. Saul's men came, and Michal said, "Well, he's ill." She had fixed the bed so it looked as though David were asleep. When the men reported to Saul, he said, "You know, I don't care whether he is sick or well. He is going to die. It doesn't matter. Bring him to me in the bed."

When the discovery was made that Michal had deceived the soldiers, Saul reprimanded his daughter. And then she lied, "Why, David would have killed me if I hadn't helped him escape." Saul's anger now had a reason. He said, "David was trying to kill my daughter. I'll get him. Get all the army! Double the reward! Go get him, men!" Michal had compounded David's problem. (Notice that David first lost his job, and then he lost his wife.). The props were coming out from under him.

AWAY FROM SPIRITUAL COUNSEL

Then David went to Samuel, his mentor, his spiritual counselor, his pastor. God protected him while he was with Samuel. The first group of soldiers came to kill him, but the Holy Spirit defended him—the soldiers began to prophesy. Another group came, and they prophesied. Still another group came, and they prophesied. Saul came, and he prophesied also! The people remarked, "Is Saul going to become a prophet? A preacher?" Then David left the spiritual guidance of Samuel; he lost Samuel. (Samuel, prop number three, removed from his life.)

Next David went to his close friend Jonathan, his blood brother (1 Sam. 20). They worked out a signal which would let David know if Saul were trying to kill him: if Jonathan's arrows went beyond him, he should keep running. As they parted, David cried out, "What have I done against Saul? I have served him as a servant and as a warrior. I have been faithful. What have I done?" (Have you ever felt like that when you began to lose? What have I done? Why did this happen to me? I don't understand this. I've been faithful; I've prayed; I've read my Bible; I've been loyal; I'm hard-working. Why did I lose my job? Why is my family breaking up? Why have I lost this friend?) Jonathan consoled him and they made a pact. David said, "Always my seed and your seed will be as family." In the end, Jonathan returned to the city; and David, a man noted for his courage, faith, stamina, and his relationship with God, ran. (Jonathan, prop number four, removed.)

Eventually David came to the city of Gath, Goliath's hometown. David found himself in the one place where he was infamously known. (David going to Gath would be like Prime Minister Begin of Israel appearing unannounced in downtown Damascus, Syria.) As he wandered around, David was recognized by the Philistines. To make matters worse, he had Goliath's sword for protection. "That's David! He killed our champion! He killed the most famous person who ever came from Gath!"

David knew that he was in trouble. So he pretended to be crazy. He began to foam at the mouth, and the saliva went down on his beard. The people took him to Achish, the King of Gath. "This is David, but something has happened to him!" Achish answered, "I'm surrounded by enough people who are crazy. I've got enough 'kooks' around me. Don't bring me a foreigner. I don't need him!" With this, David escaped. In Gath he lost his self-respect; he lost his good self-image. (Props numbers five and six removed.) Almost overnight everything he had been leaning on was removed. He was in despair and shame in a foreign country. *All he had left was God.*

GOD ALONE

Every year I see teenagers graduate from high school and leave home. They have been active in all church activities while living at home. They would remark freely about believing in God and about living for Jesus. But when they find themselves in a new environment, away from those familiar securities of family and friends, one of two experiences occur. I have seen some fine, gifted, vibrant young people slowly move away from God. They did not mean to do it. It just "happened." But when they found themselves "on their own," then true colors were revealed.

DAVID: AFTER GOD'S OWN HEART

Others, who were rather casual about their church life and their relationship with Jesus Christ, felt the need to grow deeper in him when they found themselves in a new and different situation. When all the "props" were pushed away, they leaned on the Lord alone. God is strong enough for all of our needs: *My grace is sufficient for you, for my power is made perfect in weakness* (2 Cor. 12:9, NIV). Upon what are you leaning? A better question—upon *whom* are you leaning?

On the Mount of Transfiguration, Peter saw Elijah, Moses, and Jesus. He suggested, "Let's build three tabernacles." Then the fog came; Elijah and Moses were gone; and the Bible says that Jesus stood alone: preeminent. *"They saw no man, save Jesus alone"* (Matt. 17:6). And that is how he wants to stand in your life. The second commandment says, *"I the Lord thy God am a jealous God"* (Ex. 20:5). He wants us exclusively for himself. Exodus 34:14 tells us that *"The Lord, whose name is Jealous, is a jealous God."* He is jealous of all competition. God will take every life and sooner or later pull away all the props. Joy comes when we cry, "Lord, I now lean totally upon thee."

David went to that cave in Judah. He had lost his position, his wife, his spiritual counselor, his best friend, his self-respect, and his self-image; but he went back to Judah to the Cave of Adullam. There he turned his life over to the Lord again. He rededicated his life, to use good evangelical terminology (Read about it in Psalm 34.) He repented and turned to him; he put his full weight on the Lord. "I am alone. I can't stand the icy wind of the world. I've lost everything I was leaning on." And God said, "Ah, now David, I'm ready to use you in a mighty way." You see, God cannot use some of us because our lives are already so full that he cannot put his riches into us. He cannot give us his blessings. We are so weighed down with second-best that he cannot give us his best!

There is a famous painting which depicts a chess match. The devil, portrayed as a man with horns, tail, red suit, and pitchfork, is playing a game of chess with a young man. Studying the pieces on the board, the devil appears to have won. Checkmate! The young man, perspiring profusely, is trying to find a move, but there is no way out. He is defeated. Years ago, a master of the game of chess was invited to view the painting and to see if he could discover any possible move which the defeated young man could make. He sat before the painting for over three hours until finally he saw one move: one way out of the dilemma. "Oh, young man, make *that* move. Make *that* move," he shouted before the painting.

God is in the process of pulling all the props out from under your life. Everything on which you are leaning must go until you stand before him, recognizing that every other avenue leads to defeat. As you stand before him, he says, "Oh, young man, young woman, adult, child—make that move!" And "that move" is to Jesus Christ. Lean totally on him!

6
So You Want Revenge

1 Samuel 24

He said to his men, "The Lord forbid that I should do such a thing to my master, the Lord's anointed, or lift my hand against him; for he is the anointed of the Lord" (1 Sam. 24:6, NIV).

Three little "blue-haired" ladies from South Carolina decided to take a vacation in New York City. This trio had never been to the "Big Apple," but they had always wanted to go. So finally they decided, "We're going to do it." They made all their plans and reservations and informed their families who, of course, were tremendously concerned about this threesome in the big city. With an eye toward changing their minds, well-meaning relatives reminded the three elderly ladies of the muggings and murders that routinely occur in that city. Undaunted, the ladies proceeded with their plans. When they arrived, they enjoyed all the tours and activities they could crowd into a day. They even had their pocketbooks double-strapped over their shoulders. After two or three busy and safe days, they all relaxed and observed, "Well, maybe everybody isn't killed who goes to New York."

Then one evening, as the sun was going down and they were rushing into their hotel, they ran into an elevator as the door was about to close. As they stood against the back of the elevator, advancing in their direction was an immense man with an equally immense Doberman pinscher by his side. The elevator door closed behind him and the man said, "Sit." Immediately and obediently these three women started to slide down the back of the elevator in response to the command.

Visibly shaking as they sat down, they looked up at the man. He looked at the three ladies, and the puzzled look on his face turned into a smile. He began to laugh as he said, "Ladies, not you. I was talking to my dog." As he helped them up and they were standing together again, they began to laugh uncontrollably and embrace each other. Finally the man said, "Look, I want to know you. My name is Reggie Jackson, and I haven't laughed this much in years." Rumor has it that this famous baseball player took them out to eat, and also paid their hotel bill and all their expenses for what turned out to be the time of their lives for three Southern ladies.

Now it is obvious that these women misunderstood the message Reggie Jackson delivered in that elevator. They were certain that his message had been for them and never even thought that it might have been for his dog. It was a simple misunderstanding. As we study the life of David we see how clearly he understood Saul's passion in life. Saul became obsessed with his desire to kill David, and David was aware of this obsession. It is one matter for someone to want to kill you, but it is an even more sobering thought to have the most powerful man in the country, backed by an entire army, out to get you. This is precisely what happened to David. It was when Saul hurled the second javelin that David figured out the king meant deadly business. There was no misunderstanding. In a short period of time all the props were knocked out from under David. He lost his rank, his wife, his counselor, and his best friend. Then finally, in Goliath's hometown David relinquished his last shred of dignity and positive self-image as he pretended insanity in order to escape the wrath of King Achish of Gath.

As David continued to run, he was relentlessly pursued by Saul and his army of three thousand men. At one point when Saul appeared to have David cornered, a battle broke out on another front that caused Saul to digress from his pursuit of David. But after that Philistine rebellion was quelled, Saul again turned his attention to the dominating factor of his life—David had to be killed.

DAVID: AFTER GOD'S OWN HEART

While hiding in the cave of Adullam, David recommitted his life to the Lord. Four hundred renegades and misfits had rallied around him, and David began to invest his life in those young men who had no home and no flag to follow. Soon two hundred more came until finally David had six hundred men under his command. They operated more or less as Robin Hood and his "merry men." Notice how this military exercise was preparing David for the years ahead.

The cat-and-mouse game continued until Saul heard that David was hiding in one of the caves at Engedi. One cave there is large enough to hide 300,000 troops easily. David was hiding up in the rocks and Saul came in pursuit. It was hot! Saul's men were looking everywhere for David; David and his men were hiding in the back of a dark cave. Then, of all the caves in the area, Saul chose that cave in which to "relieve" himself! *The Living Bible* says *to go to the bathroom.*

David's men said, "An answer to prayer! The providence of God! David, you've been praying that you would be vindicated. David, we have been praying that you would become king. This is it! God has answered our prayers. There's Saul!" What a vulnerable position! What a time for David to do battle with Saul! Saul didn't know that David was anywhere around. David's men kept saying, "Go get him!" David began to sneak forward with his sword in hand. But somehow he could not seek revenge. Quietly he took Saul's robe, cut off a corner of it, and went back to his men. Saul never knew that anybody was around! (see 1 Sam. 24:1-5).

OPPORTUNITY MISSED?

How unusual! How unusual in any day, especially in that day, for a man to have an opportunity for revenge and not follow through. Revenge is a vicious word. Harboring down deep within many of us is the attitude, "My day will come!" Some vengeful thought comes to mind from time to time against that person who has used, mistreated, or embarrassed us. Perhaps the event occurred years ago, yet we recall the experience and want revenge. "I'll show him! Someday I'll get the chance." Many of us have taught our children to handle adversity with a vengeance. "If somebody hits you, you hit them back twice as hard!"

What does the Bible say? In Romans 12:14 and following, Paul speaks a very clear word about revenge.

> 14 *Bless them which persecute you: bless, and curse not. Recompense to no man evil for evil.* 17 *Provide things honest in the sight of all men.* 18 *If it be possible, as much as lieth in you, live peaceably with all men.* 19 *Dearly beloved, avenge not yourselves, but rather give place unto wrath: for it is written, Vengeance is mine; I will repay, saith the Lord.* 20 *Therefore if thine enemy hunger, feed him; if he thirst, give him drink: for in so doing thou shalt heap coals of fire on his head.* 21 *Be not overcome of evil, but overcome evil with good.*

We are to overcome evil with good! Now that sounds like good "church talk." But when we try to practice this teaching where we live and work, it is not that easy. Maybe we could return *silence* for evil. "I will just ignore him." But the Bible says that we are to return *good* for evil. Jesus said, *Pray for them which despitefully use you and persecute you* (Matt. 5:44), and, *Blessed are ye . . . when men . . . say all manner of evil against you falsely, for My sake* (Matt. 5:11).

The most difficult task which I have as a Christian is to pray for and to genuinely love those who abuse me. Human nature is not inclined in that direction. Paul says that when we act in this manner, we "heap coals of fire on his [our enemy's] head." As a child, I liked this verse because I thought it meant the fire would burn them, but that is not the meaning.

The picture Paul presents is of a person whose fire went out, and so he had to borrow coals from his neighbor. A good neighbor would give him coals heaped in an earthen pot. They would put a pad on the pot so that, as the man put the pot on his head and carried it home, people would remark, "Hey, that fellow has a good neighbor." *Heaping coals of fire* is a symbol of a person who has helped someone else. When we return good for evil, we are identified as people who are going the second mile to assist those who need help—even though they have harmed us!!

Romans 12:19 says, *Vengeance is mine*. Revenge belongs to God. There will be a payday, but we are not to take God's vengeance and make it our own. David would not make God's

DAVID: AFTER GOD'S OWN HEART

vengeance his. He had a chance to kill Saul. Just one slash with his sword and he would be king! David determined that he would wait on the Lord. We get into trouble when we do not wait on God . . . when we move out with our own strength. "I'll take care of it. I know how to do it." David determined that he was God's man; he had a heart for God, a life committed to God, and he knew the commandment, *Thou shalt not kill,* was still valid. Therefore, he could not kill God's anointed. God put Saul on the throne, and God would take Saul off the throne. David would not do it.

David's men could not understand why he didn't kill Saul, but what a beautiful opportunity to teach the ways of God. Many times we have had the occasion to teach those who are away from Christ how to respond to evil—and have failed. We are to love the unlovely, to forgive those who mistreat us. When we do this, we witness to others.

SALUTE THE BARS

After Saul left the cave, David made a remarkable move. He walked out and called, "Oh Saul, my Lord." He praised Saul and showed respect and reverence for the king. He bowed down before the king: the king who was trying to kill him, who had deceived him, had lied about him, and had been pursuing him for years. He bowed before the king! Because he respected Saul? No. Because he honored the position which Saul held.

When I was in ROTC years ago, we had a commanding officer who was the most obnoxious human being I have ever met. I cannot think of a good point about him. A friend of mine declared, "They may throw me out of this institution, but I'm never going to salute that man." And somebody explained, "You don't salute the man; you salute the bars."

David honored Saul's status, so he bowed before the king of Israel. Then David delivered one of the most magnificent addresses ever spoken to an earthly monarch. To paraphrase David: "Oh Saul, I have confidence in you. You're the sovereign of God, and I have respect for you. Incidentally, you just went into a cave where I was hiding, and I could have taken your life easily. But I didn't do it, and to prove it, I want to show you your robe." He held up a piece of Saul's robe, and I have a feeling Saul looked down and saw that the piece indeed came from his own robe, and exclaimed, "Well, it is my robe. You cut my robe!" And then David brought the name of God into the conversation. He said, "I am but a dead dog and a flea. I'm powerless; I don't have any prestige. (See 1 Sam. 24:8 *ff*.).

Then he invoked again the presence of the Lord and challenged Saul to let God handle the situation. "Saul, God is going to make the decision." David spoke a word of subtle rebuke to Saul about the fact that from a wicked life there comes a wicked life-style. (What I am is demonstrated in how I live and what I do. You cannot separate these two things.) Saul could not believe the response.

When David had finished speaking, Saul replied, "Is that you, David?" Previously Saul had called him David, the son of Jesse. But now he spoke of him in a personal way. "David, is that you, my boy, my protegé? Is that you, my son-in-law? Ah, is that your voice, David?" Then the Bible indicates that Saul wept. Saul continued, "David, you're more righteous than I am." What Saul should have said was, "David, you're righteous, but I'm wicked." But he didn't say that. He said, "You're just a little better than I am." He didn't get down to the bottom line and admit, "I'm wicked." And he remarked, "David, someday you're going to be king. When you're king, David, I want you to show mercy on my family." And David agreed (See 1 Sam. 24:8 *ff*.).

THE INADEQUACY OF CONFESSION

They parted. Saul left and David went back into hiding. This was a wise move for David. In 1 Samuel 26, we find that Saul once again was chasing David. Late at night Abner and Saul were sleeping in the middle of the circle of soldiers. David crept through all the ranks of Saul's troops and took Saul's javelin (which was stuck in the ground) and his container of water. Then he went outside the camp, climbing upon a rock and looking down on the sleeping soldiers. "Saul, wake up!" he shouted. All the army was stirred and Saul awakened. "Saul, Abner, here's your spear and here's your canteen. I could have killed you again! You still pursue me." Saul responded as he had at Engedi. "Oh David, I've played the fool. Oh God, forgive me." As I read the life of Saul, I am absolutely amazed at how many times he confessed his sin. In fact, I don't know of a single personality in the Bible who confessed sin more often than Saul. He wept and cried and agonized over sin, but *Saul never did repent!!*

I have seen a man so ashamed of his sin that he would go down on his face in the dirt and cry, "I'm not low enough." He tried to dig a hole in which to put his face. I've seen that! But that man, even though he was ashamed and trapped by his sin, never turned from his sin and never repented.

Many insincere people come to church—weep and cry and agonize, "Oh God, I'm so ashamed. Oh Lord, make things right." They confess and confess; they cry and agonize, but continue to live the same old life! They never come to know God in Jesus Christ. A person can go through all kinds of physical and spiritual gymnastics of being ashamed, embarrassed, and mortified for their sins. But unless they repent, all of the tears do absolutely nothing. When we come to God, not only must there be confession, but there must also be repentance! I must be sorry enough for my sin to turn from it and turn to God.

GOD FORGIVES DEAD SIN

God forgives only dead sin. He never forgives living sin. We are good at confessing, "Oh, I want to know you, God. I want your best. I want to be obedient. I want to know your promises. I want to be in the church. I want all the feelings of joy. I want cleanliness in my life." That comes at the price of repentance and then obedience, but we must pay the price of repentance and then obey God. Saul never understood this concept! Christ comes and fills us with his Spirit when we confess and repent. Confession must lead us to turning from that which dragged us down into the mire.

Saul was Phi Beta Kappa in confession but knew nothing about a steady walk with God. Nothing about it! A person can bawl, "Oh, I feel guilty; God help me." Then they can continue the same kind of vulgarity, hatred, and bitterness which has been in their life. They will hang onto the relationships and habits which have kept them away from God year after year. There must be repentance and shame as we turn from our sins and walk in the ways of God!

As I was walking on the beach one night, I glanced down into the sand and saw something I could not believe. It was dark and I was alone; but there in my mind's eye I saw the body of my best Friend. I looked at him, and he had obviously been murdered. My closest Friend. My dearest Friend. Ah, what a man! Always doing good, always kind, always generous, always helping those who needed to be helped. Never a thought for himself, and there he was—murdered and lying in the sand. As I looked closely, I could see where cruel spikes had been driven through his hands. I could see that the same thing had happened to His feet. I looked at his brow where thorns had been crushed down upon his head. I saw stripes on his back, still red. His body was so emaciated that it looked as though he had not eaten in months prior to being murdered. I could not understand why anybody would kill this man—my Friend!

There in the night I could feel the presence of the murderer. I knew he was there; I could feel him there amid the sound of the waves and the darkness. I reached out to find the murderer, the person who killed my best Friend. Then I discovered that the murderer was nearer to me than my own hand. I tried to grasp the murderer. Suddenly I yelled, "Ah, now I've got you! I've got the one who killed him!" only to realize my hand was on my own chest. The one who murdered him was living in my heart and life! My sins cried, "Crucify him!" My sins nailed those spikes into his hands and his feet, put those thorns on his brow, and thrust that spear into his side! I was ashamed enough to turn from my sins, to repent of my sins, and to ask him whom I had murdered with my sins to cleanse my life with his blood. Who am I—Who are you—to judge any man?

Vengeance is mine, saith the Lord. In the face of evil, return goodness and love. David knew that opportunity and expediency are inadequate grounds for God to waive this principle and precept. Saul always thought his position gave him license. Confession was Saul's forté—the lack of repentance, his downfall. Be still—look at your life. Be honest before the Lord. Are you more like David or Saul?

7

How to Marry a King
(Be a Good Cook!)

1 Samuel 25

Abigail lost no time. She took two hundred loaves of bread, two skins of wine, five dressed sheep, five seahs of roasted grain, a hundred cakes of raisins and two hundred cakes of pressed figs, and loaded them on donkeys (1 Sam. 25:18, NIV).

Jesus didn't get along with everybody! That fact is both a comfort and a challenge. It is a comfort because we do not get along with everybody either; a challenge because it reveals another aspect of his life that has rarely been considered: Jesus was the revelation of God on the cross with his nail-pierced hands. The question is: Was Jesus any less a revelation of God in the temple with those same hands holding a whip?

The president of a university, among his other responsibilities, was assigned the task of garnering large endowments from wealthy people and foundations. Many times he was embarrassed by a young professor on his faculty who had often told the dreadful truth at the wrong time. This president was skilled at winning friends and influencing people, but the young renegade professor prided himself in always telling "the truth." Sometimes the clear, unabridged truth was embarrassing to the president and to the university. The president asked the professor to attend chapel on one occasion when he planned to speak. "Look, I want you to attend. I think maybe what I'm going to say today will be helpful to you."

The president's address was on the tact and diplomacy of Jesus. He talked about Jesus' utilization of the parables and his way of identifying with people. The president walked out with the young professor who said, "Doctor, I got the message this morning. I think I learned a great deal from what you said about Jesus' way with people, but I have only one question. If the Master was so tactful and diplomatic, how did he happen to get himself crucified?" Now, that is a good question! Consider the story of Jesus' cleansing the temple.

ANGER AND SIN

Jesus saw the unholy unity between the Sanhedrin and Caiaphas. He saw the moneychangers, the animals, and birds. All the merchants were hustling their wares, and the house of God had become a bazaar instead of a place for worship, praise, and prayer. Jesus took a coiled whip in his hand and began to turn over the tables. The money clanked onto the floor, the animals panicked, and all the merchants fled. He cleansed the Temple because, he said, "This is a den of thieves! And the common man who comes here to worship cannot because you have turned the house of prayer into a place of dishonesty" (see Matt. 21:12 ff.). So there we see Jesus—angry and upset. And it comforts us to know that sometimes we can be angry and still not sin.

If Jesus were to watch some of the "electronic" preachers who spend more time hustling money, promoting trips, and trying to build their own programs and egos than preaching the Word, would he go into some churches and studios with a whip and clean house? Instead of preaching the gospel, they spend considerable time promoting so they can get money to keep on promoting in order to keep their broadcasts on the air.

When I lived in the mountains of western North Carolina, there was a radio preacher who preached from a little three-watt station. He began every broadcast by saying, "Hello, world!" Then he would comment, "The old clock on the wall is moving so rapidly, I haven't even got to my text yet, but you gotta keep sending in your money so I can stay on the air." For what? I think that Jesus would look at some of these religious individuals, and he would make a whip and turn over their tables as they play on the good religious motives of the poor and ignorant.

Be ye angry and sin not (see Eph. 4:26). It *is* possible. But the truth of the matter is that most of the time when we lose our tempers, we cannot classify our anger as "righteous indignation." Usually we are defending old number one—ourselves. Someone walked on my turf or put ME down or irritated ME. Most of the time when we become angry and violent we wish that we could catch the words and put them back into our mouths. Normally when we are angry, we sin!

ANGER AND A PICNIC LUNCH

Yes, David was a man after God's own heart. He is quoted more *in the New Testament* than any other Old Testament personality. We know as much about his life as we do any other individual in the entire Bible. David's life demonstrates so many beautiful traits, yet, David became angry over a rather trivial matter (1 Samuel 25).

There is a modern proverb which states, "You can tell the size of a man by what makes him angry." Ordinarily I handle big, disastrous situations fairly well. The house burned down. There was an automobile accident. I was reasonably cool. I can handle tremendous problems and pressures with considerable ease. But let a little gnat come by and I am violent! You are probably the same way. Some people get upset at everything—big things and little things. At least I narrow mine down to little things! Perhaps I am like David at this point.

After David left the Cave of Adullam, he went into the area of Carmel and there, with his 600 men, engaged in guerrilla warfare. Saul led the army of Israel in formal battle against the Philistines. He fought all the big battles for the nation, but David would shore him up on the fringes. As he was running from Saul's wrath, David and his 600 young men battled many of the wild tribes which still had strongholds in Israel. David worked "undercover" in the mountains. His personally trained men were effective and efficient in battle. They also protected people who were grazing their flocks in that area.

Now Nabal, a wealthy man, had 3,000 sheep and 1,000 goats grazing in Carmel. David's men formed a hedge around Nabal's flocks and his possessions. After awhile, David heard that the sheep had gone back down to the home pasture where they were being sheared. During the shearing time, the owner of a flock would be generous to those who had helped in the care of his animals. This was a custom, not a written agreement.

The practice was similar to our custom of tipping. Recently, after I had checked into a hotel, the bellman came in with my baggage while I was talking on the telephone. He hung up the clothes bag, placed the suitcase, and neatly arranged a few other items. He was busy checking the thermostat, making sure the bed was just right, and checking the bathroom. But he waited until I got off the phone. When I finished my call he asked, "Is there anything else, Sir?" Now there is nothing in writing which says I had to tip the man, but it is customary. We leave a tip in a restaurant, and some of us delight in doing this when service has been rendered satisfactorily. This practice has been around for a long time! The conflict between Nabal and David was over tipping.

While David and his men guarded the flocks, they didn't lose a single sheep: none of Nabal's possessions were lost as long as David's men formed a wall for twenty-four hours a day around his herds. The time came for Nabal to tip David and his men. David instructed the men to go down and explain to Nabal who they were. He told them to: "Greet him in the name of David. Explain what we have done, and ask if he could help with our food." They were hungry! (Providing food for his men was a challenge for David.)

And what did Nabal say? He replied, "Who is David? Who is the son of Jesse? Am I to take care of every renegade, every person who runs away from his master? Am I to feed and clothe them? Who is David? I'm not going to give him a thing!" Now, Nabal was well-named. The word "Nabal" means "fool." *The fool hath said in his heart, There is no God* (Ps. 14:1). And Nabal lived as if there were no God. He pushed David's men away, and they returned and reported to David. David was furious; his auburn hair shook as he shouted, "Get your sword! Get your horses; we're going to wipe out Nabal and all of his household; we'll kill every one of them!" The troops started for the house of Nabal. (I think 400 would have been enough to kill the family of Nabal, don't you? Talk about an overkill!)

But Nabal had married a woman named Abigail. Though he was a fool, he had married *right*! The Bible says that Abigail was intelligent and beautiful. Both of these qualities combine in a charming woman, which is the term used by many commentaries to picture Abigail.

James Barrie, the Scottish author, describes one of his female heroines as a person who has charm. He states that charm is a sort of bloom on a woman. If she has it, she needs nothing else; and if she does not have it, it does not matter what else she has! Abigail had it! But what a mistake her marriage was. She did not make the mistake. Rather, her mother and dad did. Marriages were planned by the parents. So the parents of Nabal, who were descendants of Caleb—prestigious, godly, affluent family—made an agreement with Abigail's family. We can picture Abigail's parents saying, "You know, Nabal is a rascal, but he is going to grow up. He's a fool now. He's a selfish and vicious man, but he's going to grow out of it. He has to because he has so much *money*!"

How many marriages have been manipulated by parents who overlooked all the faults of a young man or woman because their parents were prestigious! Nothing else matters: "Well, she's not the best-looking thing in the world, but you can buy the best kind of misery you've ever known, so marry that girl!" Marry that guy! Many marriages have taken place just like that. And as the marriage of Abigail and Nabal, they end, or endure, tragically! We cannot blame Abigail for picking Nabal—her parents did!

When Nabal's servants heard that David was coming with swords drawn and plans to kill him and all his household, they went to Abigail and urged, "Let's go and hide. This is your chance to get rid of him." Now this must have been a temptation for Abigail. She could have come back with, "Well, you know, that's a pretty good idea. I think I'll go hide and pray for the rascal." But she didn't. Instead, she stood up for her man.

She went into the kitchen and whipped up a little picnic lunch. She put together 200 loaves of bread, two jugs of wine, five dressed sheep, five measures of parched corn (maybe popcorn), a hundred clusters of raisins, and 200 cakes of figs. Then she had them load them onto the donkeys. Then Abigail went out to meet David and his men who were coming down the mountain with swords flying and shouting, "He'll remember who David, the son of Jesse, is!" When Abigail met David, she jumped from the donkey and fell down in the dust before him. Eight times she said "My Lord" and six times she said, "Your maidservant." She honored him!

In her words to David, we find tact and diplomacy, a petition to God, and a plea to David's conscience. She said, "As king of Israel, you do not want to be remembered as a man who avenged himself against a nobody like Nabal. My husband is foolish. Everybody knows he's dishonest. He has a vicious tongue, and he speaks without thinking. You don't want to kill a selfish rascal like that! That would be no credit to you, the future king of Israel." She spoke with charm, graciousness, and sincerity which stopped David—with all of his wrath—dead in his tracks!

At that moment a tremendous characteristic of David emerged: he was teachable. He was willing to learn from a woman whom he had never seen before and about whom he knew nothing. Abigail was a nobody, a nonentity. Are you like that! Can somebody off the streets teach you anything? Or are you too good to learn? Are you above that? Can somebody without your credentials, finesse, culture, or position teach you something in a moment of your anger? Would you be willing to listen and to learn?

When David heard the speech of Abigail, he prayed, "Thank you, Lord. Blessed be to God." To Abigail he said, "You have kept me from doing something which would have permanently scarred my life." I like that! A nobody teaching a somebody! You can recognize a great man by how he treats little people.

David received the gifts, and Abigail returned home to find Nabal drunk. He was celebrating over the money he had made from the wool, and so Abigail went to bed. Abigail prayed and called on God. The next morning she told Nabal what she had done, how she had saved his life. She did it modestly, I believe. But the Bible states that God struck Nabal and his heart turned to stone. In other words, he had a stroke. Ten days later Nabal died. When David heard about Nabal's death he said, "Blessed be to God!" He said what he felt. Most people would have said, "Mmmmmm, I'm sure sorry to hear about that." David was candid. He exclaimed, "Blessed be to God." David once again walked away from revenge. God handled Nabal in the divine time schedule.

David remembered the widowed Abigail and all the food she had given him. "You know, that was the best fig cake I have ever tasted in all my life!" And he wrote out a marriage proposal and sent his servants to Abigail. It took Abigail about a New York minute to answer yes! She took her five favorite handmaids, went to David, and she married David.

CHARM AND BEAUTY: WITHOUT OR WITHIN?

How do you marry a king? Some people would surmise: Be a good cook! This story is like a fairy tale, isn't it? Abigail was married to a despot, an Ebenezer Scrooge, a mean, cantankerous man. When he died she married David, soon to be king of Israel. How to marry a king? Be a good cook.

But there is more! What if you are already married and you did not marry a king? What do you do? Simple: make a king out of your husband. How? Be a woman of God! That was Abigail's secret. *Cultivate in your life the fruit of the Spirit* (see Gal. 5:22).

Let's suppose Earl Campbell goes to his coach and remarks, "Coach, I'm one of the best backs in the NFL, and I don't like all this preseason training. It's going to be hotter this year than it's ever been before. So I'll tell you what, Coach. Because I'm the best, I'm going to show up for the first game. I have to make some more television commercials, and I just don't have time for football until the season starts." So, Earl Campbell shows up for the first game. He goes in for the first offensive play and the team runs a new "trick play": Earl Campbell into the line. He is tackled behind the line. He gets up slowly, as he always does. Then he goes back to the huddle, and the quarterback tries another one of Houston's "trick plays": pitch to Earl and he sweeps to the right. Just as he gets the ball a linebacker drills him at the waist, and a little defensive back runs through him, and at the same time a huge defensive end blasts him to the ground—Whooomp! Earl gets up and limps over to the bench. He has a muscle pull and the doctors report they don't know how long he'll be out.

We can draw one of two conclusions from this imaginary episode. Some uninitiated viewer would say that the game got

Earl Campbell out of shape. Or you could say the game revealed that Earl Campbell was out of shape. I think this second statement is correct.

Many people have the idea that the person they married messed up their life. No! That person didn't do it. The marriage revealed what was wrong with their life in the first place. The biggest problem in marriage is selfishness! And no one in this world has kept me from doing what I want to do more than Jo Beth, my wife. Nobody. And what she has not kept me from doing, my boys have kept me from doing. It is the same with you. Everyone who is married could make the same observation. It is your mate. It is your children. Because of selfishness in our lives, we blame those around us for keeping us from doing what we want to do, and therefore when problems come we always blame them. (You will never make a king out of your husband until you manifest queenly fruit in your life.)

Many times I have heard a wife say to me, "I want to talk to you, but I think I'm going to cry." And she cries. When she gets through, she says, "I don't think you can help me because Bill is not here." Isn't that some kind of statement? "I don't think YOU can help ME because BILL is not here!" Now, I'm not trying to help Bill. I thought I was trying to help her. I cannot do anything about Bill. Bill is not there.

All of us have the idea that someone else is the source of our problems. Mark 7:15 states: *Nothing outside a man can make him "unclean" by going into him. Rather, it is what comes out of a man that makes him "unclean"* (NIV). It is never the person we married, our circumstances, the city in which we live, or our vocation which is the problem. Proverbs 4:23 says your heart . . . *is the wellspring of life.* Those thoughts and attitudes which are within us reveal what we really are. The fruit of the Spirit comes from my heart—not from my mate!

From our hearts come love, joy, peace, longsuffering, gentleness, goodness, faith, meekness, and temperance! (see Gal. 5:22). Understand that! Most of us live on the basis of the flesh, and therefore we have all sorts of excuses for our problems. Nobody can make me angry. They just reveal the anger that is within me. Nobody can make me lust. They just bring out the lust which is

DAVID: AFTER GOD'S OWN HEART

already in my heart. Nobody can make me vicious, because the viciousness is there already! Nobody can make me do anything or be anything unless that thought is already in my heart. So, the problem is a heart problem! We must begin in our hearts where we find the fruit of the Spirit—or the lack of it.

Visualize a three-act play called *Marriage*. *Act One:* Two actors, two personalities. A man and his wife. The man is loving, warm, and accepting. He marries a women who is loving, warm, and accepting. They will enjoy one another.

Act Two: A man is looking for warmth, love, and acceptance. He marries a woman who is looking for warmth, love, and acceptance. What is going to happen in their marriage?

Act Three: A woman is warm, loving, and accepting; and she married a man. Period. What is going to happen in their marriage?

Complete each act of the play for yourself. But mark it down— you get from marriage what you take into it. If I have received Jesus Christ as my Lord and Savior, and if I am walking in the stream of the Spirit of God, and if in my life there is evidence of the fruit of the Spirit, then whatever happens externally, I'll have the resources to see it through. There is victory instead of defeat when Jesus Christ lives within a heart. He is the answer for our sin and deficiencies, and for our inadequacies and inconsistencies.

How can you be married to a king . . . or a queen? Good cooking is fine, but having the fruit of the Spirit operating within your life is the secret.

8
It's Windy at the Top

2 Samuel 1—5

17 *And Abner had communication with the elders of Israel, saying, Ye sought for David in times past to be king over you:* 18 *Now then do it: for the Lord hath spoken of David, saying, By the hand of my servant David I will save my people Israel out of the hand of the Philistines, and out of the hand of their enemies* (2 Sam. 3:17-18).

A man was buying a piece of property in the Los Angeles area. His realtor told him, "The three most important things to consider when buying property here are location, location, and location." You might say that the three most important things in any organization are leadership, leadership, and leadership.

How many times have we heard the expression, "All we need is the right leader"? In every walk of life, people are looking for leadership. "If we had the right person over that territory it would just catch fire with profits." "If I could find the right foreman . . . " "Ah, if only I could find a manager who would do the job." People in every walk of life are crying out for leadership, for someone to take over, to take responsibility, to take charge, to make the right decisions.

No sooner had we gone through the trauma of Watergate than ABSCAM defamed the halls of government. In addition to these, there have been multiple sex scandals which have ruined the careers of some of our most trusted men. Even more appalling has been the conduct of professional athletes who have been convicted of the use of drugs. These are our heroes, to whom we pay millions of dollars. They are supposed to represent the epitome of young manhood. They are purported to have reached the American dream.

The question has become crucial: "Is there a leader?" "Is there a prophet?" "Is there someone who has integrity?" "Is there someone—anyone—who can stand up under the spotlight?" So many times we elevate individuals to positions of responsibility who prove inadequate for the task. Suddenly they find themselves in a place of leadership in government, business, or athletics, only to discover that they do not have what it takes to be effective. One by one these inept leaders tragically fail. How desperately we need leadership.

Then there are those who are clearly qualified to be leaders but who are not willing to pay the price of leadership. They say, "It's too expensive! I'm too 'laid back' for that kind of commitment." This person has the capability of being a strong leader in his business, his community, and his church, but he simply will not put forth the effort because it is too costly. How sad indeed is such a waste of talent and ability.

There are also those who try leadership only to discover that "it's windy at the top." Have you ever noticed that? You have if you've tried to lead. If you've ever been a supervisor, a manager, or if you've ever owned a business or been president of a company, you know first-hand that "it's windy at the top." Leadership is tough at any level.

Still there are others who are not qualified for leadership, yet they scratch and claw their way to the top, only to discover when they get there that they really cannot handle the job. Then comes the sad irony of sliding back down, past all those who were stepped on, in order to get above them in the first place.

There are some flaws of character that work against effective leadership. Some of the very qualities that are required to become a leader can be so perverted that they cause a person's descent rather than his ascent. When leaders fall dramatically, whether they are leading a small business or a worldwide organization, there are common flaws and weaknesses which bring them down and render them useless as leaders.

One homiletician suggested that we remember these danger signs of descent by the letter "S." They are Silver, Sloth, Sex, and Self. The course of the demise can be traced back to one of these words. He either lets greed (Silver), laziness (Sloth), immorality (Sex), or pride (Self) destroy him. With these potential impediments to leadership in mind, let us look at the life of David as he accepted the role of leadership God had for him.

David began a new place of leadership after the death of Saul. (Remember Samuel had anointed him to be king years prior to this.) Immediately at Hebron, he was made king of Judah, his own tribe. King over one tribe!

DAVID, THE LEADER

The *first* quality of leadership was that he commended the past. He praised Saul, his predecessor. He was able to distinguish between Saul the man, the friend, the father-image, and Saul the king who could not rally Israel and be obedient to God at the same time. David saw the good qualities in Saul, commended his name, and honored him. What an important trait in a leader! Many people get to a position of leadership and responsibility and then spend all their time belittling those who have gone before, in order to lift themselves up. How we need to be able to look behind us and compliment the past, sort out the good, and move forward. David had a forward vision for the people, but he had wisdom to understand that it was right for him to praise what had gone before. That, I think, is the mark of a secure leader.

Second, David was a praying leader. He was only thirty years old as he began his reign, but he turned to God in prayer. He said, "Oh, God, I must have your wisdom." And God instructed him to make Hebron his capital in the southern kingdom of Judah. How we desperately need deacons, teachers, leaders, and business people to pray to God, to be people of the Book, and of petition and intercession. David knew that he had to have supernatural assistance.

In the *third* place, David had a way of commending his enemies. Some of us have the idea that in order to lead, we draw a line and say, "Zip, you're for me or against me, and if you're against me, get out of the way!" Not David! His first act as king was to send messengers to Jabesh Gilead, a hundred miles from Hebron. (That was a long way!) His message to the people of Jabesh Gilead was one of "kindness and faithfulness" for taking care of the body of Saul and Jonathan in an honorable fashion before they could be buried as anointed of God. Jabesh Gilead did not forget David's blessing.

For seven-and-a-half years, while David was king only in the southern kingdom, Abner was the primary leader of the other tribes. David tried to help that son of Saul and to keep the remainder of the kingdom together. Finally Abner came to the conclusion that David, and only David, had the qualities of leadership. He told the people, "In times past you have tried to make David king." (He was implying that David had prevented this from happening.) "Now is the time. Do it now. Do it now!"

How many times in our own lives we have tried to make Jesus Christ king. But we have procrastinated. We have said, "Let's wait." Is the Holy Spirit of God saying to us, "Do it now! Make him king. Make him ruler over your life." But there are many things we must straighten out. There is so much territory that has been taken over by the enemy, the "Philistines" of this world. The secular world controls us. We can wait for awhile (or can we?).

ENEMY ATTACK

As we read further in the Scripture, we see that David was attacked by his enemies immediately after he became king of all Israel. *The Philistines also came and spread themselves in the Valley of Rephaim* (2 Sam. 5:18).

When we say, "Lord Jesus Christ, I want you to be Lord of all; I want you to be sovereign in my life," we are attacked afresh by many of our old enemies. The devil comes and bombards us; he knows every point of weakness, and he attacks us on all fronts. When we make Christ sovereign, we enter into new areas of warfare. As long as we co-exist with sin, Satan is happy. But when we say, "Lord, I want you to be supreme in my life," spiritual warfare erupts. The longer I am a Christian, the more areas I recognize as not being under the control of Christ. As he moves into another area, here comes another battle. The devil does not surrender and say, "Well, come on in and take over."

As Abner said, "Do it now!" So the Holy Spirit says, "Do it now! Make him Lord of all. Make him sovereign. Make him supreme." At first the idea of being controlled by the Holy Spirit is frightening. But the victory is surely in Jesus Christ as he permeates every area of our lives.

GREAT DAY

The people of the northern kingdom saw in David the qualities which they wanted in their king. One of the great days in the history of Israel was when David united the kingdom. In actuality, never had this been accomplished before. Saul had been king, but the children of Israel controlled only little villages on tops of mountains. From the time of Joshua, they lived a hand-to-mouth existence under the watchful eye of the Philistine nation. The Philistines controlled the fertile valleys and had the water. Because of their incomplete victory years before, the Israelites had lived on top of the mountains from Joshua's day.

Finally David came into leadership, and he controlled all of the land. *All* of the land! Well, he controlled all the land except one little spot, right in the middle of the territory. There was one place which never had been captured. Jebus! The Jebusites had three hundred acres and a fortress which never had been penetrated. Sargon had looked at it across the years; Sennacherib had looked at it. But they did not attack. When David was made king, he said, "I'm going to control all the land; we will take Jebus."

The people were caught up in the tide of patriotism and exclaimed, "Let's go, David. We'll take Jebus!" This city was a citadel in the cliffs—a natural fortress. As David and his men approached Jebus, the guard saw the army coming. He shouted, "We don't have time to kill you boys today. But we have some blind and lame soldiers who will do the job. They can take care of you and we will bury you in the morning, David." The military men of Jebus laughed at David and his ragtag army as they surrounded the fortress of Jebus.

Their laughing at David was a mistake! (He probably remembered laughter from his older brothers, Eliab and Shammah, and his father, Jesse.) David responded, "We'll take Jebus!" Jebus fell

DAVID: AFTER GOD'S OWN HEART

to the forces of David. An amazing military victory! As I read the Bible, I wanted to find out the details of that battle, but we know almost nothing about it! Somehow he got his men through a water conduit which went into the city, and in one fell swoop, the Jebusites were defeated. That is all we know. It was a phenomenal victory! David did not assault the cliffs of Jebus in Cecil B. DeMille fashion. David was the kind of military leader who would take his soldiers in, win the victory, and bring his soldiers out. General George C. Marshall in World War II had this same kind of ability. There have been very few generals like that. Many generals know how to win but do it at the expense of the blood of their troops. (General Patton was an example of this type of leadership.) Not David! His military insight has never been duplicated in all of history! (see 2 Sam. 5:6 ff.). Ask the men at West Point, "Who was the greatest military leader in the history of the world?" Many will agree that it was David, the biblical personality, because of what he did with what he had.

David even stole from the Philistines their ability to smelt iron, a feat which no one else was able to do prior to that time. He became a mighty military warrior, captured Jebus, and killed the Jebusites. They had been a thorn in the side of Israel since Joshua and Caleb came out of the wilderness and possessed the Promised Land.

"Okay, David, you're king. You have Jebus. What are you going to do with it?" David said, "If I put my capital in the south, at Hebron, the north will be upset. If I move the capital of the nation to the north, my own people who have supported me will be upset. What will I do? I'll make it Jebus" (see 2 Sam. 5:9). This was a place which never had been controlled by an Israelite, a place few Hebrews had even entered except to trade—and then, they had left before nightfall. David called his new capital "Jerusalem." Then he decided that if this were the capital of God's people, he had better go and find God.

CLEAN HANDS—PURE HEARTS

God and the ark were synonymous so he sent his men to Baalah in Judah to get the Ark of the Covenant (see 2 Sam. 6). While they were gone, David arose before daybreak. He took his stylus and a piece of clean slate and went out on a mountain there in Jerusalem. As he climbed he reasoned, "The ark is coming. I will put in on this hill overlooking the whole city. God is in that ark. God is alive in the midst of his people in that ark! I will write a hymn for all the people to sing as the ark is coming up Mount Zion." And he wrote Psalm 24: *The earth is the Lord's, and the fullness thereof: the world, and they that dwell therein. 2 For he hath founded it upon the seas, and established it upon the floods.*

Now someone will say that this is David's cosmology. But the statement concerns more than his belief about the origin of the earth. Of course, he was saying, "God made the sea. God placed the foundation of this world. God put the seas in the middle of it. God is a part of all this." His cosmology was also his theology. He sang, "God made the sea which I drove the Philistines into. God made the brook where I picked up those stones. God made the stones. God made Goliath. God made *me*!" That is what he believed about God!

Then he began to think of God and the ark. "Who will be worthy to go and worship the Lord, to stand before the cleansing radiance of God?" Then he asked that tremendous question: 3 *Who shall ascend into the hill of the Lord? or who shall stand in his holy place?*

Who around is able to ascend the hill of the Lord, to climb Zion, to look at God, to speak with God, to know God? He had the answer: 4 *He that hath clean hands and a pure heart; who hath not lifted up his soul into vanity, nor sworn deceitfully.* Someone who is honest, who has clean hands. The psalmist says that we must have a clean heart; our motives, our reasons, our rationale, our meditations must be pure. Those who have clean hands and a pure heart can climb the hill of Zion and reach for God! Therefore, nobody is qualified to climb that hill!

"What can I do to qualify? Surely there is some work that I can do." No—you start by *being*. The blood of Jesus Christ penetrates the deepest habit, the ingrained sin, that garbage to which you return, over and over again. You must turn from these habits, these deadly sins, and allow the blood of Jesus Christ to permeate the deepest recesses of your life and take that territory which is controlled by the enemy. God wants to be sovereign over all your

DAVID: AFTER GOD'S OWN HEART

life. Because of the cross, by the forgiveness of Jesus Christ, and the filling of the Holy Spirit—and not of your own strength—you become cleansed by his grace and forgiveness. Then you can stand before God! *Justified* by Jesus' blood!

Josiah Wedgewood was a man greatly skilled with pottery, and also a man of God, moral man, clean man, upright. Once a nobleman came to the shop where he molded that priceless pottery in the old days. He asked a fifteen-year-old boy to show the nobleman around. The boy was showing the visitor all the tools and the method of pottery making, the glazing, and the intricate system which required so much time and skill. This nobleman was a profane man. At first the boy was bothered by his language, but the man was so effervescent and so vulgar that the youngster began to laugh at him and to admire him. Josiah Wedgewood made no comment but followed along quietly.

When they finished their tour, Wedgewood dismissed the boy. Then he picked up a piece of prized pottery and explained to the nobleman how long it took to make the piece of art and how much it was worth. It was a priceless piece, a collector's item. As he reached to hand it to the nobleman, Josiah Wedgewood dropped the pottery, and it shattered into countless pieces on the floor. The nobleman could not believe it. He was furious. "Why did you do that? I wanted that priceless piece for my collection!"

Wedgewood said, "Sir, in time, with effort and labor, that piece of pottery can be remade. In fact, I can make a better piece than that one. But, sir, there are some things which cannot be reconstructed once they are destroyed. And you, sir, today have scarred the simple faith of a boy who had great reverence for God. You, sir, have profaned sacred things with your speech in his presence."

The problem in the world—in America—in so many lives of those who even go to church fairly often is that we have profaned sacred, holy things. Therefore, our hands and our hearts are not clean and pure. Unless we commit our lives to Christ for forgiveness and cleansing, we never will be ready to climb the hill of God, nor will we be ready to take on the area of responsibility which God has in mind for each of us.

It's windy at the top. See you there?

9
Qualifications for Building God's House

2 Samuel 7; 1 Chronicles 17:1-27, 22:8; 1 Kings 8:18

1 *Now it came about when the king lived in his house, and the Lord had given him rest on every side, from all his enemies, 2 that the king said to Nathan the prophet, "See now, I dwell in a house of cedar, but the ark of God dwells within tent curtains"* (2 Sam 7:1-2, NASB).

Have you ever committed yourself to the Lord and after a time of prayer and waiting on him, had a vision about something you should do? You begin to dream a worthy dream, maybe even a holy dream. You feel that this idea is of God, and not blind ambition. But as you put this dream into reality, God says, "No." God's "no" can come through another person, through a roadblock in circumstances; it can come in many shapes or forms. But that "no" halts the reality of your dream. How do you handle that "no" when it comes into your life?

Look at the circumstances. Israel was at peace. During this time of tranquility, David could sit back and think about his accomplishments. David had Nathan at his side. (Who our companions are at times of rest, relaxation, and recreation is an important matter!) While David was with Nathan, the prophet and man of God, he had a vision: he wanted to build the temple. He had built his own house. "I have a lovely house of cedar, and now I have a dream that the ark will not live in a tent, but in a beautiful temple. I want to build a place for the people to worship."

3 *And Nathan said to the king, "Go, do all that is in your mind, for the Lord is with you"* (NASB). Nathan must have been a Baptist! Have you ever heard of a preacher who turned down anyone who wanted to build a church? David said, "I have this vision of a beautiful church, a place of worship for the ark."

Nathan the preacher said, "This sounds great to me! Do it with all your heart. It's right! It is of God. Go and do it."

GOD'S ANSWER

> 4 *But it came about in the same night that the word of the Lord came to Nathan, saying, Go and say to My servant David, "Thus says the Lord. Are you the one who should build me a house to dwell in?"* (NASB).

And in verses 5 through 16, God speaks to Nathan and instructs him to say to King David, "You are not to build the Temple." God said *no* to the goal of David's life—his dream, his vision, a high and noble purpose. But with this *no,* he gave David words of encouragement. He reminded David of his blessings upon his life. "David, I want you to remember that I found you when you were following sheep. And I protected you and led you victoriously through all the conflicts which came in your life. Now you have defeated all of your enemies. You are on the throne of Israel, you control this whole area, you rule over all my people. You cannot build the temple, but one of your descendants will build it."

In 1 Chronicles 17, we discover that God said no to David, "but one of your descendants will be qualified to build the temple. I will use *you* as a warrior king. Your family will be known forever." And we know that all of these words came to pass. Through the lineage of David, Jesus came, in the fullness of time, as the Messiah.

How did David respond? How did you respond when God said *no* to you? Did you sulk or did you seek? What happened when you said, "I'm in love—That's the one for me," but that *no* came? How did you act? "That's the vocation I want to pursue." But God said, "No, you can't do it. You're not equipped to do it. This, instead, is what I want you to accomplish." Have you thought, "If I had my choice to do anything in the world, I would like to be this," but God did not give you the mental capability to do it? God's *no* comes to good people, even concerning worthy things. How did you respond?

15 *According to all these words and according to all this vision, so Nathan spoke to David.* 16 *Then David the king went in and sat before the Lord* . . . (NASB).

Immediately after God said *no,* David went to the Lord in prayer. He sat before the Lord. And then in the next three or four verses, we see that David counted his blessings in the form of questions. He asked questions of God which God had just answered.

" . . . *Who am I, O Lord God, and what is my house that Thou hast brought me thus far?"* (NASB). God just told him, "You are the king: a special king." "What is my house?" God had just told him about the promise to David's descendants.

18 *"What more can David still say to Thee . . . For Thou knowest Thy servant"* (NASB). "I was a shepherd; now you have made me king. What more can I say? I'm speechless!"

A certain businessman loved to hunt but he kept getting lost in the woods. On his birthday, his office staff gave him a pocket compass. Shortly thereafter, he got lost again. When they asked him why he didn't use the compass, he said that it couldn't be trusted. He started walking north and tried to set the needle in that direction. But the thing wouldn't go. It kept shaking and shifting to the southeast. It is easy to get lost in the perplexity of life, and to come into situations again and again where we don't know which way to go. Sometimes God will say, "Go right" or "go left," or he will answer *yes* or nothing. Perhaps God's most difficult word to accept is *no.* When God says "No," he wants to deal with you in a special way: perhaps in a way in which he never has worked before. That *no* gets your attention! And when David's overwhelming *no* came, he ran to God.

David was before the Lord in a child-like fashion of humility. Verse 18 says, "What more can David say?" At a certain age, our children ask questions which they seem to be asking for someone else. My boys did this. Cliff would say, "Can Cliff have some ice cream?" He was not asking for himself; he was asking for "Cliff." "Is it all right if Ben goes outside?" In other words, the child is thinking, *If it's not all right, and the wrath comes . . . well, I'm just asking for someone else!*

David counted his blessings in humility before the Lord, and he

DAVID: AFTER GOD'S OWN HEART

was speechless. In a spirit of prayer, he was submissive before God, and ready to listen. From verse 22 to the end of the chapter, David speaks beautiful words of praise. How long has it been since you have been quiet and still with nobody around—no noise or TV or movement—and said, "Oh, Lord, look at my life and evaluate it"? When you are before him in this manner, you will be overwhelmed at what God has done in your life and where God has brought you.

"And now, O Lord God, Thou art God, and Thy words are truth, and Thou hast promised this good thing to Thy servant" (2 Sam. 7:28). For the first time in his life, David began to claim personally the promises of God.

NO AND GOD'S PROMISES

When God says "No" and we go to him in praise; we count our blessings; we are humble before Him; then, in a spirit of prayer, we claim the promises he has for us. God never says No . . . period. He always asks, "Now, what do you need?"

"Well, I need forgiveness." *I have blotted out, as a thick cloud, thy transgressions* (Isa. 44:22).

"I need inner peace." My peace I give you, I do not give to you as the world gives. Do not let your hearts be troubled and do not be afraid (John 14:27, NIV).

"Lord, I'm worried about whether or not I'll go to heaven." *I go to prepare a place for you. And if I go and prepare a place for you, I will come again, and receive you unto myself; that where I am,* [That is in heaven!] *there ye may be also* (John 14:3).

"I need holiness. I need to get my life right." *Be ye therefore perfect, even as your Father which is in heaven is perfect* (Matt. 5:48).

"Really, I need guidance." *In all thy ways acknowledge him, and he shall direct thy paths* (Prov. 3:6).

So, what do you need? All the promises of God are waiting for your claiming. Psalm 37:4 says, *Delight yourself in the Lord and he will give you the desires of your heart* (NIV). God will place desires within us as we walk in him. What he wants for us becomes what we want for ourselves. Isn't that something!

QUALIFICATIONS FOR BUILDING GOD'S HOUSE   79

WHY?

David never asked, "Why?" That would have been my first question! We had prayed that my father would be healed, but he died. I remember going out into the park behind my house at that certain trysting place where I had often met with God. In the beginning, I asked, "Why?" But as I prayed and talked with the Lord, I had the comforting assurance that my earthly father was with my heavenly Father; and, suddenly, I was in a spirit of praise and weeping and laughing before God.

Evidently, David did not know until later in life why God would not let him build the Temple. First Chronicles 22:7-8 recounts David's instructions to Solomon, his son who would be king and who was qualified to build the Temple.

> 7 *David said to Solomon: "My son, I had it in my heart to build a house for the Name of the Lord my God. 8 But this word of the Lord came to me: 'You have shed much blood and have fought many wars. You are not to build a house for my Name, because you have shed much blood on the earth in my sight'"* (NIV).

Finally, David discovered why God said *No.* "You have blood on your hands. You have been a warrior king. That was your purpose in life."

Stand outside a church with beautiful stained-glass windows. When you look from the outside, the windows look like ordinary windows—nothing special. They are dark and without significant form. You cannot tell exactly how they look because the light is behind you. But from the inside of the building, you look toward the light. Then you see beautifully colored windows: scenes from the life of Jesus, pictured from Old Testament history, magnificent in color and detail. It all comes together because you are facing the light.

So many times as things happen in our lives, the light of God is behind us. We look at these events as dark and foreboding: a dead-end street. But perhaps there will come in our lives a time when we can look back and face the light of God. Then we see the situation as beautiful, and we understand the meaning of that *no.*

IN YOUR HEART: IN YOUR HAND

First Kings 8 tells of the dedication of the Temple after it was completed by Solomon. 17 *"My father David had it in his heart to build a temple for the Name of the Lord, the God of Israel. 18 But the Lord said to my father David, 'Because it was in your heart to build a temple for my Name, you did well to have this in your heart'* " (NIV).

Do you know what that means? God credited David with having built the Temple! When David died, the Temple did not even have a foundation. But Verse 18 says that God gave David—not Solomon—the credit for building the Temple, because he had it in his heart. What a profound insight! When we open heaven's records, we find that David is credited with building the Temple, not Solomon. How can this be? God's way of measuring success and failure is totally different from our standards! That is what it means. God looks on what we would have done if we had had the ability and opportunity, more than he considers what we actually did in our lives.

The world does not measure success like that. The primary standard of the world is: deliver the goods! Make the sale! Move the product! Promote the corporation! Achieve! Oh, there is talk of procedure and protocol, of ethics and integrity, but the bottom line is, *Deliver the goods!* God looks at what motivates us; he sees our hearts! Mark 9:35 says, *If anyone wants to be first, he must be the very last* (NIV).

Jesus said, *He that humbleth himself shall be exalted* (Luke 4:11). The great people are the humble. Before you reject the paradox, consider how much the thoughts of men have come over to this view. This insight of His about the proud and the humble, so incredible in that age of despotic power, has now become the virtual consensus of mankind. Humility was not a virtue in David's day or in Jesus' day. It was a servile attitude, demanded only of slaves. But today, generally speaking, we do not admire the proud and arrogant. We no longer stand in awe before the pomp of kings, nor are we impressed with pompous people who elbow their way to chief seats. We have come to admire humility and modesty, even when we do not personally possess it. David humbly submitted to God's resounding *no* and yet the Bible says God rewarded him as if a green light had been given.

Henry Pipkin felt that God was calling him to be a missionary to

China. He prayed and studied through high school, college, graduate school, and seminary. He learned the language and the dialects, and finally he was appointed and went to China. On the day he landed, the Boxer Rebellion began. He was in China for only an hour or two and was killed. He never won a person to Jesus Christ in that land; he never helped one person on that mission field; he never preached one sermon. Now, the world would say of Missionary Pipkin, "He didn't do anything for God."

But I have a feeling that when we get to heaven and those books are opened, we will see Henry Pipkin's name in glowing reports. There will be hundreds of thousands of people whom he touched for the Lord Jesus Christ. I think that Pipkin would say, "Look, Father, I failed. I got myself killed when I landed on the mission field. I didn't do all of this." Then God will answer, "Ah, but you had it in your heart to do it! You were ready. You were motivated; therefore, you are credited with being a great man of God in China."

The way God evaluates a life is different from our scale of measure. This insight should encourage many people! Some people say, "You know, if I were able, I'd give a million dollars to the Lord."

"I wish I'd gone to the mission field. I felt the tug and I wanted to serve in that capacity." "If I were able to teach a class . . . " "If I had started that business or had bought that land . . . " "If I had married that person or had moved there . . . "

There were *ifs* in our lives—and *no's* which came through a person, an economic situation, a tragedy.

But how can I *know* what I would do if I had the chance? Consider David. He spent four decades as king, gathering materials for a temple which he would never be able to build. Read about it in Chronicles. He collected gold, silver, cedar timbers. He found craftsmen. He made bricks and cut stone. He had the ideas and the plans. Then David handed everything over to Solomon and told him what to do.

What happens to us when we are not on that committee—not in a prominent place—not "in on" all the details? We criticize, find fault, whine, and complain. So often within our hearts we say,

DAVID: AFTER GOD'S OWN HEART

"I'm not leading; therefore, I'm not for it! I won't give to it, and I certainly won't celebrate."

David's attitude was so different! He knew that he would never see the Temple, but he had it in his heart. How can we tell what big things we would do if we had a chance? We can look at what we are doing with that which we have in our hands right now. What are we doing with the abilities and talents God has given us? We must measure what is in our hands right now! We must live right now—not in the past or in the future. "Oh, Lord, this is what I have. Use it. It is in my hands; it is yours."

When Jesus recognized the biggest offering ever given in the New Testament, it came from that little widow who gave what she had. *I tell you the truth,* He said, *this poor widow has put in more than all the others* (Luke 21:3, NIV).

To find your life, you lose it. Those who are first in this world may be last. Those who are last could well be first because God looks at our minds, our hearts, and our motives. What he finds there is credited to our divine account. What are you doing with your abilities, talents, dreams, ambitions? God says *No* so we will get into the Book, claim his promises; and then he opens new vistas of endeavor in our lives.

In everything you do, put God first, and He will direct you and crown your efforts with success (Prov. 3:6, TLB). His success is the only *real* success after all!

10
The Mid-life Tragedy: Adultery

2 Samuel 11

In the spring, at the time when kings go off to war . . . (2 Sam. 11:1, NIV).

When Alexander the Great was at the pinnacle of power, he invited a famous artist to paint his portrait. The painting depicts Alexander the Great with his head in his hands, as though he were thinking. However, historians tell us that Alexander had a horrible scar on one cheek, which he had received in battle. Since he was ashamed of the scar, he had the artist paint him with his hands covering it.

Make no mistake about it. The Holy Spirit, inspiring the authors who penned the Book, never once attempted to hide the scars of any Bible personality! All the blemishes and shame are revealed clearly for all of us to see. Even David, who was called the man after God's own heart, is seen in all his sordidness and sin.

CONSEQUENCES OF A LINGERING LOOK

In the spring, at the time when kings go off to war . . . David was at home in the palace! In the afternoon, David took a nap. He got up, stretched and yawned, and walked out onto the balcony; and he surveyed his city, the capital city. As he looked he saw a breathtakingly beautiful woman. In the Hebrew, you do not see this particular descriptive phrase used often. Evidently, she looked like Venus de Milo, Helen of Troy, and Cleopatra, with the countenance of the Mona Lisa. In our modern vernacular, she was a "10"—at least!

David looked and saw her bathing. And his look lingered, and it precipitated into lust. He sent an inquiry and received an answer. Then he sent a command, and she came; and he slept with her. Afterward, there was duplicity, lying, and murder.

Some have tried to blame Bathsheba by asking, "Why was she taking a bath on a balcony in the afternoon?" Bathsheba was not guilty because that was the time when Eastern women took their baths! All the men were out in the fields, either at war or protecting the city. The people would catch rainwater in cisterns on the flat roofs. While the water was warm from the afternoon sun, the women bathed. It was the natural thing because there was no men around—oh, except for David, the king, God's man. (Remember now, David was not a rogue; he was not a rascal. David was a shepherd, the psalmist, God's anointed king.)

Bathsheba returned home, with no one the wiser. Time passed, and one day a messenger took David a note: the note that will make strong men tremble; that will turn the most astute, masculine man alive to butter; that will make ice water flow in his veins, and at the same time, bring sweat to his brow. The note read, "I am pregnant.—Bathsheba." What would David do? One of the functions of the king was to enforce the Law of Moses. And the law was clear at this point: If any man and woman be found in adultery, they are to be stoned to death. The man *and* woman. The king was to carry out the law.

THE COVER-UP

David knew immediately that there must be a cover-up. "We'll have to take care of this. Why, this can't happen to me, the king. I'm special; I'm different; I'm David." Quickly, he sent for Bathsheba's husband, Uriah the Hittite, one of David's own commanders, and one of the thirty-five "King's Men." These men were hand-picked by David and had been in all the battles with him. "Send for Uriah the Hittite. Have him come and give me a report from the war."

And so Uriah came in and talked about the battle and other military matters; then David asked about Joab, the general. After a while he said, "Uriah, you might as well spend the night here. I'll see you in the morning. Go home and wash your feet, have a delightful meal, and spend the night with your wife."

Later in the evening, David sent a gift to his house. Ah, it was perfect! The story would be simple: Uriah came home, and a child was born. No one would question that! Everyone would remember the time when Uriah came home from the battlefield.

The next morning, David discovered that Uriah did not go home, after all. He had slept with David's servants outside, by the king's door. David asked, "Uriah, why didn't you go home?"

"Oh, King, I could not go home when the ark is out on the battlefield. (Remember, the ark was God, to them.) And when my general, Joab, and all my friends were sleeping out there under threat of their lives. I couldn't spend the night at home because I am one of the King's men: I'm one of your men, David. I couldn't go home while they're out on the front line!"

Uriah was some kind of a disciplinarian, wasn't he? What a military man! Who taught Uriah to be this kind of man? David. Until then, David had lived like that too. David had known always that in the springtime kings go out to war, and war was serious business.

And so, David carefully tried again. "Uriah, stay another night." This time, David got him drunk, which is a sin in the Old Testament, incidentally. Still Uriah did not go home. He spent the night outside with the servants.

David must try something else; he had to approach the problem from a different angle. He wrote a note instructing General Joab to put Uriah's company on the front lines: to send them on a suicide mission so that Uriah the Hittite would be killed. That was the only answer! Now, who would take the note? Why, he would send it by Uriah, himself. And Uriah delivered the note which led to his own murder. What trust David had in Uriah the Hittite! Uriah the Hittite was certainly a man of God, a man of integrity, and a man of brave patriotism and loyalty.

Not only was Uriah killed, but perhaps the whole company was killed so that General Joab could cover up his defeat. When the messenger returned with the news of how they lost the battle, David was so benevolent. The messenger did not understand, but David said, "You go back and tell General Joab, 'You win some

DAVID: AFTER GOD'S OWN HEART

and you lose some. That's just the way it is with war!' You tell General Joab to go back out and attack again and again, and he'll be victorious. God bless him, the Lord be with him."

Weeks went by. After the appropriate time of mourning, David called for Bathsheba. In a very charitable way, under the guise of loyalty to the memory of Uriah as one of David's thirty-five hand-picked commanders, David asked Bathsheba to be his wife. Can't you hear David say, "Her husband has been so faithful to me through all these years of conquest it is the least I can do"? All the people applauded. "What a great king we have, to be so concerned about the wife and family of one of his commanders!"

The marriage took place. Nobody knew; nobody suspected—except General Joab; he couldn't be fooled. But he wouldn't tell. The servants may have thought—but who would challenge a king who had never known defeat? The king who had brought the nation together, who had written and sung all those glorious songs; a man who was a national hero; who had brought prosperity to God's people; and a man who had established the capital city; who built his own palace; and who was making plans to build the Temple of God? Who would challenge such a man?

Months passed. Surely this was the perfect crime. David, the genius, the man of strategy and insight, had taken care of the crisis in his brilliant way.

A CONVICTING STORY

But David forgot one thing; it was the same thing Moses forgot when he killed the Egyptian. It is the same thing we forget every time we fall into sin. In 2 Samuel 11, there is not one mention of the name of God, in the sense of reverence to Him, except in that last verse. And that one word carries with it tons and tons of weight. David forgot one truth, as he covered up everything else. *But the thing David had done displeased the Lord* (2 Sam. 11:27).

Who would speak to the king? God's prophet, Nathan, who was faithful and fearless, went to him and told him a story. A traveler visited a rich man, who had many flocks. Rather than kill one of his animals for dinner, the rich man went next door, to the house of a poor man, who had only one little ewe lamb. The ewe lamb was a household pet. It would sleep with the children, who loved it dearly. We would say that the lamb was a "member of the family." But the rich man stole that ewe lamb, killed it, and served it to his visitor. Nathan asked David, "What am I to do? How am I to judge the man who did this deed?"

And David became angry! He said, "Oh, the man should be killed! The rascal! Make him pay for the lamb four-fold!"

Nathan, brokenhearted, with tears streaming down his face, trembling, knowing that his words could mean that he would be killed, looked at his king and said, "Oh, David, it's you! You! It's you I'm talking about." (I have heard this scene described as Nathan shaking his fist in David's face. But I don't believe that. I am confident that Nathan spoke quietly through his tears.)

Suddenly, one hot blast from the breath of God came through David's mind, and his conscience and his heart. During all those months, he had grown indifferent and callous; but then David saw himself the way God saw him. And he cried, "Oh, my God, I have sinned against you."

LOOK OUT, KING DAVID!

There are principles which we will consider from this event:

Principle number one: We have referred to it before. "It's windy at the top!" David, at the pinnacle of his career, fell into his deepest sin. One commentator said that David's sin resulted from his youthful passions. Nonsense! David had been on the throne for over two decades. He was past fifty years of age at the time— middle-aged plus. I do not believe that a man has ever lived in the history of the world who had a record to match David's at this point. He had a military genius which never has been duplicated in all of history. First Samuel 5:11 describes success after success, victory after victory, honor after honor, against unbelievable odds.

In the realm of music, David can be compared with Beethoven. Consider the creative power of his pen. David the psalmist reminds us of an ancient Shakespeare. As an administrator, he trained thirty-five mighty men to be leaders in the kingdom. Israel and Judah became a people of great prestige and prosperity because of his skills in business endeavors. His political prowess united the twelve tribes into a mighty nation. As an athlete, David had equal agility with the lion and the bear as he did with Goliath. David had it all together! He was one of a kind!

David was at the height of his spiritual life as well as his secular life. He had been chosen king by God. His writings evidence deep insight into the mind and the heart of God. In an earlier chapter, we consider David's celebration and praise to the Lord when he brought the Ark of the Covenant into a newly prepared tent in Jerusalem. And his heart burned with the desire to build a house for God. David was committed to spend his energy collecting materials and making plans for the temple, even though he knew that he would not build it. This man was soaked in the blessings and guidance of the Lord. But at the pinnacle of spirituality, he fell. And what a fall! Satan uses these great spiritual times to attack us.

A man walked down the aisle of the church with his wife and family. They had come to know the Lord and were baptized into the church. Their lives came alive in the Lord as they began to pray and to read the Bible. The man's business improved; Christian friendships began to grow. There was a new style about his life; he saw things in a different light. The touch of God brought with it freedom. Everything was great!

One Sunday when he went to church, he felt the Holy Spirit in his life in an unusual way. He left the service determined to be even more committed to the Lord. Later in the afternoon, his wife took him to the airport. He had business in a distant city the first thing Monday morning. After a good-bye kiss, he boarded an airplane and settled down for the trip. When the captain had turned off the light, the man loosened his seat belt, mashed the magic button, and comfortably leaned back. About that time a beautiful young woman came by. She spoke, "Excuse me, but would it be all right if I sit by the window?" And in his mind he heard the Holy Spirit say, "Look out, King David! Look out!"

Be careful! The thoughts that the Devil would plant in our minds might find a home there. And the devil attacks when we are on high spiritual ground.

Principle number two: "No one falls into sin . . . suddenly!" David did not fall suddenly. "Well, it happened just out of the clear blue sky. He looked and saw this woman and one thing led to another!" Oh, no. Sin does not work like that—especially sin of the flesh. His path to this sin began early in the life of David. How can that be? When we read the Psalms and the book of Samuel, we see that David took everything before the Lord in prayer. Before he would go out to battle, he would talk to God. He talked to God before he decided on his leaders. He talked with God about which city should be the capital of His nation. He prayed all the time! David talked with God about everything. Well, not quite.

Not once do we find that David talked with God about his love life. Not one time! And that was the area which had plagued him. He had ignored it as it developed away from God's plan. Not one time did he talk to God about his eight wives and his numerous concubines. Deuteronomy 17:16-17 gives clear instructions as to what the King of Israel is *not* to do.

He was not to multiply his means, his silver and gold. The King of Israel was not to use his position to tax the people in order to become a very wealthy man himself.

Also, he was not to multiply his horses. Horses? Oh, yes! It was a prestigious achievement to have horses. And he would go to Egypt for more horses. He was not to return to Egypt, the land of enslavement. He was not to multiply his horses.

Then, he was not to multiply his wives: *that his heart turn not away* (Deut. 17:17). Away from what? Away from God!

David had already broken that law. He had kept the others; he was concerned with neither personal riches nor horses. However, 2 Samuel 5 tells us that when David moved his capital from Hebron to Jerusalem, he took more wives and concubines from that city.

Mark it down: One of the infamous lies which our society supports is that when a passion or an appetite is fed, it will be satisfied. That is not true! The more wives and concubines David had, the more his passion increased. The same is true of anybody, anytime, anywhere. The more you feed it, the more it will grow! This is true spiritually, as well as physically and emotionally. Did you know that the sex drive and spiritual motivation are located in the same part of the brain?

David did not fall suddenly! This sin had been building up all through the years. Think of that tree in your back yard which blew

90　　　　　　　　　　　　　　**DAVID: AFTER GOD'S OWN HEART**

over when the big wind came. Where did it crack and split? If you had taken a close look, you would have seen that little worms had bored into the tree and that disease had been rotting the tree for some time. It had been "falling" for a long time. The storm simply provided the impetus necessary to knock it over.

The Teton Dam broke and sent millions of gallons of water cascading down through the Snake River Canyon, causing the deaths of hundreds of people. That didn't just happen! There had been a little crack below the water line, which no one had seen. As it expanded, it was discovered. Someone went to repair it . . . too late. In fact, those who were to fix it barely got off the dam before it erupted. That didn't happen suddenly; it had been happening a long, long time.

Many people tolerate perversion coming slowly into their lives. Their thoughts and habits, their dream worlds, and viewing worlds are preparing for an eruption! Others are surprised when something happens—"Who would have thought . . . ?" But it doesn't happen suddenly. That episode has been building for years!

Some people do not seem to have any problems in the area of the flesh. "That doesn't bother me!" Paul says beware if any man stand, take heed lest he fall. *" . . . if you think you are standing firm, be careful that you don't fall!"* (1 Cor. 10:12, NIV). Thus, Paul gives us warning. Look out, King David, look out!

Unless God is in the picture in every area of our lives, we are in trouble. But thank God, He is in the picture with David! What David did displeased the Lord. Surely he would say, "David, look what I've done for you! I have given you the kingdom with all its prestige. You were a nobody, and I made you a somebody. Since you have turned away from me David, so will I turn away from you." But you see, God does not give up on us easily.

> 7 *This is what the Lord the God of Israel says: "I anointed you king over Israel, and I delivered you from the hand of Saul. 8 I gave your master's house to you, and your master's wives into your arms. I gave you the house of Israel and Judah. AND IF ALL THIS HAD BEEN TOO LITTLE, I WOULD HAVE GIVEN YOU EVEN MORE* [caps mine]. 9 *Why did you despise the word of the Lord by doing what is evil in his eyes? You struck down Uriah the Hittite with the sword and took his wife to be your own. You killed him with the sword of*

the Ammorites. 10 Now, therefore, the sword will never depart from your house, because you DESPISED me and took the wife of Uriah the Hittite to be your own! (2 Sam. 12:7-10, NIV).

God would have given David more! But David "despised" the Lord.

THE LOVE OF GOD

These are not the condemning words of a judge spoken to someone who has fallen into sin. They are the words of a lover who's heart has been broken! God's heart had been broken. And He was saying, "Oh, David, I love you still. I love you still."

The duplicity in David led him to overcompensate for his sin. He seemed so pious. One step led to another. He treated Uriah with such favor; David sent him home to be with his wife. Later, he gave the messenger a word for General Joab, "You win some and you lose some. Keep fighting and God will give you victory." Then he became violent when he heard Nathan's story.

How we overcompensate for our sin when it is unconfessed in our lives! When we see sin in somebody else's life, we criticize and condemn. We seem to be "above" sin. We imply the idea that we have been measured for our wings! Then we hear that voice, "Look out, King David! Look out, King David."

If we listen closely, we can hear a voice from the cross saying, "I don't care what you have done. I know all that, but I love you still. I want you to come back to Me and to be clean again." We remain in sin simply because we will not receive the forgiveness of God in Jesus Christ! Beware of the thought the devil tries to plant in your heart because it *could* take root.

"Oh, I'm too old for all of that. I'm middle-aged!" Look out, King David, look out!

11
Pressure!

2 Samuel 12:1-15*a*

But the thing that David had done was evil in the sight of the Lord
(2 Sam. 11:27, NASB).

A year passed between David's sin and his confrontation by
Nathan. Weeks turned into months, months into years. David
forgot to keep a short account with God. He pushed all of his guilt
into his subconscious. He did his best to hide it deep in his heart.
He rationalized. He tried to explain it away. But unconfessed guilt
and sin always appear in some other way, in an unusual disguise.
Have you noticed that?

David seemed to do okay. No one ever mentioned what
happened. Read Psalm 32, penned during that year. He had
health problems and emotional problems. 3 *When I kept silent,
my bones wasted away through my groaning all day long. 4 For
day and night your hand was heavy upon me; my strength was
sapped as in the heat of summer* (NIV). No matter where David
went, he could not escape. He was caught! The hand of God was
upon him.

HOW TO DEAL WITH SIN

How do you deal with sin and guilt in your life? What do you
say when nothing is right and you cannot find the problem? Do
you say, "I'm tired!" or "I'm frustrated!" or "I'm not myself"? Do
you run from quiet moments? The TV must be on or some project

underway. We want to have someone around or we must be reading or planning. Because in those times of silence, the Holy Spirit comes and reminds us that we are grieving God. We do not like the quiet moments!

Maybe you handle sin the same way you handle that little red light that appears on your automobile dashboard. You pull off the road, lift the hood, and look intelligent to impress your wife. Then you say, "You know, it's serious." You creep over to the next exit and go to a service station where a magnificent mechanic will fix your car—for only $523.43!

Or when that warning light flashes, you can ignore it. The scenery is beautiful; you are in a hurry; so you do not pay any attention to it. Maybe you are cruising along and you simply do not see it.

Or you could carry a little hammer in your glove compartment and when the red warning light comes on you think, "I don't like red lights!" so you get out your hammer and—"Whoooomp"—you break out that bulb. It does not blink any longer! Then you say, "Everything is great." There is only one problem: you keep on driving and your motor burns up! Some of us handle guilt and sin in our lives just that way.

There is a warning; there is a pull at your heart, your conscience, your emotions. Confused, you put the thought out of your mind. There is a warning light from God. You find it in church when someone speaks or reads from the Bible. You try to pray and God is not there. So you take a hammer and break it out! And if you go on and on as David did—for weeks and months—your life will burn up. You feel like the drought of summer has sapped all your energy and strength. Sexual sin will do that more than any other kind!

A year passed, and the warning came. God was displeased. *Then the Lord sent Nathan to David* (2 Sam. 12:1, NASB). *"Then the Lord . . . "* Where had God been? What does this mean? In God's own time and according to his schedule, he came into the picture. When did God enter the picture? After David sinned with Bathsheba? No. After David killed Uriah? No. After Uriah and all of his men had been killed? No. Did God come into the picture following David's marriage to Bathsheba? No. Or when their child was born? No. *Then,* after David had been weighted down by his sin for all those months, after he had wallowed in the mire of frustration, after he was caught up in his own lies, hypocrisy, and chicanery—*then* the Lord appeared on the scene.

God has a way of not only saying the right word to us but saying it at the right time. I do not like God's timetable many times! I implore, "Lord, what more do we have to do?" "Do it NOW!"

"God, why do you wait about this thing?" "Do it NOW!" God knows the right time to touch a life!

Then God spoke to David through Nathan. The story about the lamb, which the prophet told, had a special impact on David (story in preceding chapter). What did Nathan do? He had a clear word. Wonder why Nathan used a lamb? Could it be because David loved lambs? The shepherd boy had been a part of the birth of those lambs, and he had carried lambs. The shepherd loved the sheep! And David was angry at the rich man: "The man deserves to die . . . He will have to repay four-fold."

Nathan, with brokenness, said, "You are the man." David replied, "I have sinned before the Lord." Then Nathan told him, "David, you will not die due to the fact that your sins have been covered." David repented of his sins.

REPENTANCE: GOD'S INITIATIVE

Many times we have the idea that we can repent when we want. That is not true. Some people say, "I can come to know God and Jesus Christ anytime I decide." Not true. Some say, "Well, I can confess my sin and receive forgiveness anytime I want." That is not true. Repentance must come before forgiveness and cleansing from sin. The reason many people have prayed for days and years concerning sin—sometimes the same old sin—and have never found spiritual victory is that they never have come to the place of godly, biblical, grieving repentance.

In Acts 11, there is the account of Peter telling the elders of the church that the Gentiles have come to know Jesus Christ. Verse 18 states, *And when they heard this, they quieted down, and glorified God, saying, "Well, then, God has granted to the Gentiles also the repentance that leads to life"* (NASB). God took the initiative.

Then in Romans 2:4 (NASB) we find, *Or do you think lightly of*

PRESSURE! 95

the riches of His kindness and forebearance and patience, not knowing that the kindness of God leads you to repentance? God granted repentance, and the kindness of God leads us to repentance. Consider 2 Corinthians 7:9-10. 9 I now rejoice, not that you were made sorrowful, but that you were made sorrowful to the point of repentance; for you were made sorrowful according to the will of God, in order that you might not suffer loss in anything through us. 10 For the sorrow that is according to the will of God produces a repentance without regret, leading to salvation; but the sorrow of the world produces death (NASB). So often our repentance is not real; we have not gone through the sorrow which God brings to us. We are really not convinced that we have sinned, and if we had the same opportunity again, we would do exactly the same thing. See? When we go through godly grief, sorrow, and remorse for sin, God gives the gift of repentance.

When we are wrestling with sin (sin that has us by the throat!) we pray, "Oh, God, help me. Cleanse me from this sin. Oh, God, give me strength to defeat this sin." But first, we need to pray, "Oh, God, grieve my heart; break my heart; give me a godly repentance." There must come compassion and conviction. "Oh, God, I'm lost, undone, ashamed." There must be tears of sorrow which lead us to repentance. God grants that kind of repentance through his kindness. We cannot deal casually with sin. There must be godly sorrow, grief, and shame before we repent and turn to God in Jesus Christ. That is real repentance! A contrite heart is an honor to God.

MARKS OF REPENTANCE

David's repentance was a *real* repentance. How do I know that? He said, "I have sinned against the Lord." *First* of all, I know it because he did not offer any excuses. He did not try to explain it away. He did not say, "Well, Bathsheba should not have been walking around without any clothes on." He did not say, "Well, Uriah needed to die. He wasn't such a good commander anyway. He failed me in that battle." David did not offer any excuses or rationalizations: "Well, what happened was because of my genetic composition," or "I'm just a passionate person," or "My mother weaned me too early." He simply confessed, "I have sinned." And that is the mark of genuine repentance!

Some people cannot make a simple statement of guilt. Have you ever had somebody apologize to you in such a way that you felt guilty? I have. "You know, I'm sorry I said what I did about you. I wouldn't have said it if I'd known you were such a sensitive person." "I didn't mean what I said about you; I was just kidding. I didn't know you were so thick-headed. I thought you would understand that I was just kidding." And they think they have apologized!

We deal with God in the same way. "Oh, Lord, forgive me of this sin. You know why I fell in this sin. It's because of . . . " And we give an excuse. David showed a mark of true repentance. He cried, "I have sinned." No fine print, no conditional phrases, no rationalization. "I have sinned."

The *second* mark of David's true repentance was that he listened to Nathan and did not get angry at him. Most of the time when someone tries to speak the truth of God to us in love, we get upset and use all of our defense mechanisms. We do not want anyone to bring us to terms with God. If there is someone who loves you enough to deal with your life in a truly humble, loving, spiritual way, thank God for that person! That individual loves you and is a gift from God to keep your life right and true. It is tough when God uses *our children* to bring us before his judgment. If we listen to them, we hear them speaking some strong, strong words to our hearts. I know that his was true repentance because David listened to God's man, Nathan, as he spoke the truth in love.

Also, I know that David's repentance was real; for in the *third* place, David understood the true nature of sin. David wrote Psalm 51 during that period. *Be gracious to me, O God, according to Thy lovingkindness; According to the greatness of Thy compassion blot out my transgressions* (NASB). David used "transgressions"—a plural word. David listed all of his sins before God. I know people who never get right with God while they continue to pray, "God, forgive my sins. Oh, Lord, all the people of the universe are sinners. Everybody sins. I'm a sinner, too. Oh, forgive my sins." God wants us to be *specific* about our confession. He wants us to pray about those sins one by one. David listed his sins before God: lust, adultery, lying, murder, deception.

PRESSURE! 97

Sin dealt with effectively is sin dealt with radically. Sin is not a station-to-station proposition; it is a person-to-person proposition. And David then came to understand. He said, *Wash me thoroughly from my iniquity,* [singular] *and cleanse me from my sin* [singular] (Ps. 51:2). What is the difference? He listed all of his sins, and then he saw the true nature of his sin; therefore, he used the word "iniquity" which means "twistedness." David said, "Here are the 'symptoms' of sin in my life." One, two, three, four, five, six, seven, eight, nine—he piled all the garbage in a heap. But then he saw the truth: "My real problem is iniquity." He looked down under his sin and discovered that his sin was against God. *Against Thee, Thee only, I have sinned. And done what is evil in Thy sight* (Ps. 51:4).

"Well, David, you didn't sin against Bathsheba? What about Uriah?" "David, what about the lives . . . " "What about the unborn generations?" But David saw that the true essence of sin is always sin against God. This truth we need to teach our children. Our sin is sin against God. That twistedness in our nature leads us to do all these wicked things. We could spend a lifetime dealing with sin from every angle, but we must recognize its source. "Oh, God, there is something in me—my nature, my carnality, my unbroken spirit. Lord, I have rebelled." Our sin is not against God as a Judge, but against a God who loves us and is brokenhearted because of our sin. David's repentance was true because he understood the nature and character of sin: Sin is always against God.

FORGIVENESS

Then forgiveness came—a beautiful word of forgiveness! Nathan said, "David, you'll not die. David, I have covered your sins." There are so many beautiful phrases in the Old Testament about sin being covered, put behind the back of God, in the depths of the ocean, buried in the depths of God's forgiveness: sin that is far from us as the East is from the West. You see, the distance between the North and the South can be measured by the North and the South Poles; but the distance between the East and the West cannot be measured. Therefore, our sin is as far from us as infinity.

DAVID: AFTER GOD'S OWN HEART

All of these truths are from the Old Testament, before Calvary! Look at the promise of forgiveness after Calvary. *If we confess our sins, he is faithful and just to forgive us our sins, and to cleanse us from all unrighteousness* (1 John 1:9).

"Your sins are covered," said Nathan, "You'll live. You've confessed your sins. You've come to true godly repentance, David." I wish we could stop there! I wish we could just close that passage and say, "Isn't that beautiful? Forgiveness; light; reconciliation. He's back with God; he's forgiven; he's pardoned. God has covered his sin; no longer is sin there. The penalty is gone!" But there is more!

CONSEQUENCES

10 *'Now therefore, the sword shall never depart from your house, because you have despised Me and have taken the wife of Uriah the Hittite to be your wife.'* 11 *Thus says the Lord, "Behold, I will raise up evil against you from your own household; I will even take your wives before your eyes, and give them to your companion, and he shall lie with your wives in broad daylight. 12 Indeed you did it secretly, but I will do this thing before all Israel, under the sun."* [David confessed and Nathan told him that he was forgiven and would not die.] 14 *"However, because by this deed you have given occasion to the enemies of the Lord to blaspheme, the child also that is born to you shall surely die."*

God forgives and forgets sin; God cleanses us from our sin; He hides, He covers our sin. We are free from the penalty of sin, but there is still the consequence of sin. Why? It is because we live in a moral universe. And God does not wave a magic wand and change the whole nature and character of this world, which is built on godly, divine, moral principles. *Always* sin carries with it *consequences.* What was the consequence of David's sin? Nathan said, "The sword will not leave your house." Remember what David said that the man should do who killed the ewe lamb? He should repay four-fold! "The sword will not leave your house, David." That was the consequence, and here is the four-fold way in which David paid for his sins.

First, the baby boy was born to David and Bathsheba and lived to be perhaps three months old when suddenly he became sick and died. "The sword will not leave your house, David."

Amnon, the second son of David, raped his half sister Tamar, and was killed by Absalom because of that incestuous relationship. "The sword will not leave your house, David."

In the third place, Absalom rebelled against David, tried to kill his father, and finally was found hanging from a tree by his hair. Then Joab put those deadly darts in his heart, and Absalom died. And we still hear the lament which every father and mother understand, as David said, *O, my son Absalom! My son, my son Absalom! If only I had died instead of you—O, Absalom, my son, my son!* (2 Sam. 18:33, NIV) "The sword will not leave your house, David." And as David was dying, the fourth son, Adonijah, led a revolution against his father. Adonijah was killed by Solomon. "The sword will not leave your house, David." These were consequences of his sin.

"Why, that's biblical stuff. That won't fly in our world!" Mark it down! People all around can tell about the consequences of sin. Divorce is rampant in our society, and divorce is sin, as we all know—especially those who have experienced it. God can forgive, forget, cleanse, and put it under his blood, as he has for so many victorious Christians. But those same divorced people will testify about the consequences of that sin in the scarred lives of their children and of themselves. Sin can be forgiven, cleansed, forgotten, put behind God, buried in the ocean, but the *consequences* are there! The Bible teaches it, and we know it in life! Dissipate your life and God will forgive, cleanse, and try to restore you, but when your organs have been damaged and your health has been destroyed, those scars, that consequence of sin, remains. Always!

Do you keep short accounts with God? It is important that we do! Bring your sin into his light quickly. Keep a short account with him. Do not let the grass grow under your feet! Open your life to his light, to his forgiveness, to his love, and pray, "Oh God, give me a grieving heart. Show Your kindness to me. Give me your repentance so I might be clean."

As David prayed, so must we. David wrote, *Create in me a clean heart, O God; and renew a right spirit within me.* Lord, to my heart bring back the springtime, and he will do it—every time!

12
The Father of a Rebellious Son

2 Samuel 12-15

And the king was much moved, and went up to the chamber over the gate, and wept: and as he went, thus he said, O my son Absalom, my son, my son Absalom! Would God I had died for thee, O Absalom, my son, my son! (2 Sam. 18:33).

On the battlefield of Saratoga, a beautiful obelisk was erected to remind our nation of that strategic battle during the Revolutionary War. On that monument are four niches. In those niches are the bronze statues of the generals who fought and led in a distinguished fashion. There is the statue of General Gates, General Schuyler, General Morgan, and General . . . empty! The fourth niche has no statue, merely a base with a name, a name which conjures up memories of the history of our great nation. It takes only a glimpse at the name of this general to understand why he is no longer recognized as a hero of that war. We fail to remember his glorious victories at the battles of Quebec and Saratoga. We think only of that dark moment by the Hudson River when this general sold his nation to the enemy. His very name has become synonymous with treason in our language. "Benedict Arnold" died as an old man in a little room in London, England, friendless, penniless, with not even a family to comfort him. Benedict Arnold.

An empty monument! In 2 Sam. 18:18, we see that Absalom built a monument for himself in the king's burial grounds of Israel, in the king's valley. Because he had no children, and therefore no heir, he constructed the memorial in order to be remembered as the prince of Israel. As the king's son, he planned to become a greater king than his father David and to rule for many years. But something happened. Absalom's monument is without a body, too. Following his death, he was thrown into a deep pit because of his rebellious acts against David. As they were marching home from battle, the soldiers threw great stones over his body. Thus, he was buried like a common criminal in an unmarked grave. Contrast a pile of stones with a great mausoleum. Contrast a hero's life and burial with that of a man whose name we care not to speak.

When reading about Absalom, we ask the question, "What happened to this young man?" The Bible says his body was without blemish from his head to the bottom of his feet. He had long, flowing hair, a well-defined physique, and a quick mind. What potential this young man had! What happened?

To understand Absalom, we must look at his home and his family. In order to truly understand a child, or a man or a woman in adulthood, we must go back to his home and his roots. In so doing, we can see why Absalom failed. So many times things happen in the life of a teenager or young adult which we cannot understand or comprehend. In looking back at the events of childhood, parental and sibling relationships, we can usually find the source of the problem. That is exactly what happens as we study Absalom in light of his father David.

DAVID'S SIN: GOD'S JUDGMENT

David was guilty of a gross sin which he covered up for over a year. Finally, after being confronted by Nathan, David confessed, "I have sinned." Then forgiveness came to David as Nathan said, "You will not die." But Nathan also told him of the consequences of his sin.

Galatians 6:7,8 says, 7 *Do not be deceived: God cannot be mocked. A man reaps what he sows.* 8 *The one who sows to please his sinful nature, from that nature will reap destruction* (NIV).

Most of us like 1 John 1:9: *If we confess our sins, he is faithful and just and will forgive our sins and purify us from all unrighteousness* (NIV). We like forgiveness and cleansing, but we have the idea that because we are forgiven, because our sins are under the blood of Jesus Christ, there are no consequences of the sin we have committed. That simply is not true, biblically or experientially! The law of the harvest, sowing and reaping, is an irrevocable law. It is part of the framework of the moral universe of God. There will be a harvest of whatever we sow. We may be forgiven of the sowing of our evil seed, but the *consequences* will always follow.

Suppose a man loses his temper and gets into a fight. His opponent gives him a direct hit and breaks his nose. No matter how many times he asks for forgiveness, his nose is still broken! He is forgiven by the man who fought with him. He even forgives the man for breaking his nose, but he must have corrective surgery or go through life with a crooked nose.

The consequences of David's sin were so far-reaching because it required so long for David to get right with God following his sin. He did not keep a short account! Romans 6 tells us that we do not have to sin. We are not slaves to sin. When we sin, we are going against the Holy Spirit of God, Who has empowered us and filled our lives. He gives the Christian the power to resist all sin that comes to his life. Sin cannot overwhelm him! Therefore, when we fall into sin as Christians, we are going against the instruction and the equipping of the Holy Spirit. *Therefore,* we will reap the consequences!

From 2 Samuel 12, we have already seen Nathan's words concerning the events which David could expect because of his sin. Throughout the remaining chapters, the record of the prophecies is seen:

1. The son of David and Bathsheba would die. *So David said to his servants, "Is the child dead?" And they said, "He is dead"* (2 Sam. 12:19, NASB).

2. God would raise up evil against David from his own household. (Numerous events during David's remaining years fulfilled this word.) His wives would be given to his "companion," or family member, and he would lie with them before everyone. Absalom controlled Jerusalem for a time. He took the advice of

Ahithophel: 21 *Go into your father's concubines, whom he has left to keep the house; then all of Israel will hear that you have made yourself odious to your father . . . 22 So they pitched a tent for Absalom on the roof, and Absalom went in to his father's concubines in the sight of all Israel* (2 Sam. 16:21,22, NASB).

3. The sword would never depart from his house. Amnon, David's son and heir to the throne raped Tamar, his half-sister who was a daughter of David. She was Absalom's sister (2 Sam. 13:10,14). For two years, Absalom hated Amnon for this deed, until he had the occasion to kill him.

> 28 *And Absalom commanded his servants, saying, "See now, when Amnon's heart is merry with wine, and when I say to you, 'Strike Amnon,' then put him to death. Do not fear; have not I myself commanded you? Be courageous and be valiant." 29 And the servants of Absalom did to Amnon just as Absalom had commanded . . .* (2 Sam. 13:28,29 NASB).

Absalom ran away from home and went to Geshur. Second Samuel 13:39 says, *And the heart of King David longed to go out to Absalom; for he was comforted concerning Amnon, since he was dead* (NASB).

ABSALOM RETURNS

> 23 *So Joab arose and went to Geshur, and brought Absalom to Jerusalem. 24 However, the king said, "Let him turn to his own house, and let him not see my face." So Absalom turned to his own house and did not see the king's face* (2 Sam. 14:23,24, NASB).

After two years, David finally reinstated Absalom. (2 Sam. 14:33) But this wayward son continued taking his father's place in order to win favor with the people. *So Absalom stole away the hearts of the men of Israel* (2 Sam. 15:6, NASB).

In 2 Samuel 18, we read that David's army defeated the army of Absalom. Afterwards, Absalom was caught in a tree by his beautiful hair and was killed by Joab. When David heard the news, he went to the chamber above the gate and cried his infamous lament before the Lord: *"O my son Absalom! My son, my son Absalom! If only I had died instead of you—O Absalom,* my son, my son!" (2 Sam. 18:33, NIV). These words were uttered in the same place David's sin began: in a bedroom! Whatever we sow, we reap. There will be a harvest, and we are allowed to see the harvest time, the tragic harvest time, in the life of David: A harvest that touched and destroyed the effectiveness of his children.

PRINCIPLES FOR FAMILY LIVING

Why should we study the life of David? If David could come and speak to us in the twentieth century, I think he would say, "Learn some basic principles about family living."

The first principle is this: The secret sins of the parents so many times become the public sins and shame of the children. What parents call moderation often become excess in the child.

Where did Amnon get that lustful eye for his own sister? He saw it in the eye of his own father, the king. David reaped what he had sown. Notice how God's judgment came. It did not move supernaturally. Lightning did not strike the temple! One of the children was not killed in a chariot accident. Judgment comes in the working out of God's order in this moral universe. The principles of God are laid down and set. Amnon learned that lustful glance, which led to the raping of his half-sister, from his father, David. In fact, what Amnon did was not nearly as critical as what his father did. David's act with Bathsheba was punishable by the stoning of both people involved. Amnon, in taking his sister who was a virgin, should have been punished by either marrying her or by paying the dowery for her, under the law of Leviticus.

Where did Absalom get the idea that he could murder his own brother? Why, he remembered the strategy his father used in trying to get Uriah, the Hittite, drunk. Therefore, his plan was the same: Get Amnon drunk! Absalom did not kill his brother; his servant did. David did not kill Uriah, the Hittite; the enemy did. We can look at the lives of all the children of David and see his reflection! The secret sins of the parents so many times become the public sin and shame of the children.

The second principle in the tragic story of the home life of David is this: There is no substitute for parents in the lives of their children! David did not really know his children. In fact, indirectly he was an accomplice to all of these tragic deeds which took place within his own home. It was David who told Tamar to go and cook a meal for Amnon since he was ill. If David had known the nature and character of Amnon, his lustful son, he would have known not to put his daughter in a position of privacy in the bedroom of such a man.

It was David who instructed Amnon to go to the family reunion because he himself did not have time to go at the invitation of Absalom. So Amnon went, and was murdered by Absalom. When Absalom led a rebellion against his father, David evidently did nothing about it. Was it not David who allowed his son to march in front of a chariot with fifty footmen, pretending to be a king, drawing the eyes of the people away from the true king? David did not know his children!

So many parents today do not know their youngsters. I hear parents say, "I can't believe this about Susan" or, "I can't believe this about Bill." They had no idea what their children were involved in or what they had been doing. David neglected his children because as king of Israel, he was extremely busy.

We also see a third principle demonstrated in David's family: Children want and need attention, whether they try to get it in a good or bad way. They either want our praise or our criticism; they want something! "Don't neglect me." The opposite of love is not hate. It is indifference! A rebellious child many times is simply saying, "Notice me. Do something about what I've done." Absalom was no different.

He was brought back from exile after being with the king of Geshur for three years. For two years, David refused to see him. Finally Absalom sent word to Joab, David's right-hand man, and said, "I want to see the king." When he received no response from Joab, Absalom sent word a second time. Still, no response. So Absalom burned the crops of Joab. Now, that got his attention! He arranged a meeting between the estranged father and son.

Like all of David's children, Absalom wanted to be loved and touched and encouraged. Spend quality time with those children! Let their agenda be your agenda. Dad, where were you during the little league game which meant so much to your boy? Mom, where were you when they needed somebody to help out in the first grade? Oh, Dad had a big business deal. Mom had a bridge party. They had to play tennis. They were on a trip. Nothing in the world will substitute for your time with your children. They want to be touched and loved. We *all* want to be touched and loved! Determine how to spend quality time with your family. I have always given first priority to my family schedule and have never regretted it. Try it and your children will grow up and *call you blessed* (cf. Prov. 31:28).

A woman was in the hospital. She had a whole entourage of doctors who examined her. Finally, a diagnosis was reached. "Well," the doctor explained, "we found out what is wrong with you. You need to have your gall bladder removed. Which doctor would you like to perform the surgery?"

The woman described a doctor—tall, gray-haired man, horn-rimmed glasses. The physician immediately recognized him as the chief of surgery. He said, "You don't know his name?" "No."

"Well, why do you want him to do the surgery? You have had all of these specialists. Why him? You don't even know his name." She replied, "He's the only one who touched me every time he came in to see me. As he would leave my room, he would always pinch my big toe. I just got the idea that he really cared for me. I want him to do my surgery!"

We must listen to our children. When we do not have time to hear their silly little stories when they are young, how can we expect them to tell us "big things" when they are older?

The fourth principle: If you do not effectively discipline your children, sooner or later you will have to live with a broken heart. David did not discipline his children. Amnon raped Tamar at home, and David did nothing. For two years Absalom waited for David to do something for the honor of his sister. The father did nothing. Absalom took the matter into his own hands and killed Amnon. Absalom ran, but David did not pursue. After Absalom returned, he lived two years at the palace, but David did not have time to see him. He did nothing. Absalom won the hearts of the people by opposing his father and by telling them what they wanted to hear. David did nothing. Nothing! No discipline for the children.

With one of my boys, a firm whack in the place God provided

for sitting works the best! With another one, I have to sit down with him and reason. Just a look and my other son straightens up! We have to know our children to understand the methodology to use. We must look for the way to discipline those whom God has entrusted to us as parents. And how important it is that we discipline with love.

Many of us do discipline our children, but we are not qualified to do it! Why? Because our own lives are not straight and clean and clear and true. We cannot discipline! That was David's problem.

Notice the positive aspects of these principles. If our lives are right, publicly and privately, then we will spend quality time with our children, then we can discipline with love. And this discipline is effective!

In Boulder, Colorado, a twenty-five-year-old boy brought suit against his mother and father, suing them for $350,000 on these grounds: "You did not rear me right." If that holds up in court, I know some young people who could file suit against their parents, and any fair jury would find them guilty as charged!

David would have died for Absalom, but he would not live with and for him! We will die for our children, but we will not give ourselves to them in the formative years, in the beginning years, in the middle years, in the later years. "Oh, I will die for you—but not right now. I'm too busy; I have things to do; I have my own life."

What do we do about it? We let our children see that the Body of Christ, the church, has priority. We let our children see that we love our husbands, that we love our wives; because this is the best sex education they will ever get. We let our children see that we reverence God's Word. We let our children see that the Lord, prayer, and the Bible are more important than anything else— more important than our pleasure or our vocation! When we do this, our children will rise up and call us blessed.

Begin today! Wherever you are, begin to walk with the Lord. The blessing will come, and your children will say, "You know, my mom and dad wanted only to please God and to get God's best for me."

13

How to Forgive an Enemy

2 Samuel 16:5-13; 19:15-23; 1 Kings 2:8-10

And be ye kind one to another, tenderhearted, forgiving one another, even as God for Christ's sake hath forgiven you
(Eph. 4:32).

Do you hold grudges? Is there someone who has offended you . . . and you still remember? Think about it: that acquaintance long ago; a teacher from high school days; the girl who stole your boyfriend; a family member—your mom or dad; your boss or another person at work. Make a list of these people; you will need it later!

"But I don't have any bad feelings toward anyone!" Maybe not; but do you recall a person about whom you have said, "He got what he deserved!" Perhaps there *are* individuals who should be on your list after all.

A FORGIVING KING?

King David had a list. And what a list! In his life, David experienced one tragedy after another; all that happened to David is almost unbelievable. Think of all the people who had hindered his life! In 2 Samuel 16, we find this man at his lowest ebb. He was in the *pits*! He had never before been this depressed, defeated, and despondent. Hope was gone. This situation reminds us of the time he was in the Cave of Adullam, when Saul was after him. He despaired for his life! The sword had not left his house since his sin with Bathsheba. He faced one consequence after another.

David's son, Absalom, had led a revolution, a coup d'etat. We find him leaving Jerusalem, walking up the Mount of Olives. He is barefooted, with his head covered. As he weeps and groans, his "mighty men"—the royal remnant—surround him. Absalom has won the hearts of the people, and David believes that Absalom soon will try to kill him. At this low moment, this defeated man encounters Shimei (From 2 Sam. 16 NASB).

> 5 *When King David came to Bahurim, behold, there came out from there a man from the family of the house of Saul whose name was Shimei, the son of Gera; he came out cursing continually as he came.* 6 *And he threw stones at David and at all the servants of King David; and all the people and all the mighty men that were at his right hand and at his left.* 7 *And thus Shimei said when he cursed, "Get out, get out, you men of bloodshed, and worthless fellows!* 8 *The Lord has returned upon you all the bloodshed of the house of Saul, in whose place you have reigned; and the Lord has given the kingdom into the hands of your son Absalom. And behold you are taken in our own evil, for you are a man of bloodshed."*

David was guilty of many sins, but he was not guilty of Shimei's charges. He had tried to protect the household of Saul. Also, Absalom took the kingdom; the Lord did not give it to him. Talk about kicking somebody when they are down! When there seems to be no hope for David, Shimei came, throwing stones and cursing. He's abused David. Just look at the situation!

"Shimei's" come to all of us, don't they? After we have had the flu, here comes a "Shimei" who blasts us the first day back on the job! Have you noticed that? When everything else is going wrong, here comes another "Shimei" to tilt the scales and push us down a little further than we are. When I seem to be experiencing the darkest days of my life and the whole world is turning on me, "Shimei" begins to throw rocks at me and to abuse me. Do you identify with that? If you do not know a Shimei, stick around; you will meet several! When everything is glorious and beautiful, we don't hear Shimei. When we're down, Shimei is waiting!

At that point, David got some interesting counsel. 9 *Then Abishai, the son of Zeruiah, said to the king, "Why should this dead dog curse my lord the king? Let me go over now, and cut off his head*" (2 Sam. 16:9, NASB). Now, that will take care of the Shimei's! There is always an Abishai who advises, "The way you deal with a "Shimei" is to cut off his head. Use your ultimate force. Knock him down; beat him up; throw him out; fire him." Many people handle problems in that way. (But what if your Shimei has died? Forget about him?)

A lady became ill and checked into a hospital. The doctor made his diagnosis: "You definitely have rabies. I would advise you to make out a will as soon as possible." He left the patient for a few hours. When he returned, she had a paper filled with names. The doctor said, "You must have a lot of people you want to remember in your will."

"No, I haven't gotten around to my will yet. I'm first making a list of all the people I'm going to bite!"

Now, this was the counsel of Abishai! Probably, David's men joined in, "We'll cut that rascal's head off. Who is he anyway? He's nothing but a dog! Notice how David handles the situation. He answered Abishai: 10 *But the king said, "What have I to do with you, O sons of Zeruiah? If he curses, and if the Lord has told him, 'Curse David,' then who shall say, 'Why have you done so?'"* (NASB).

Do you know who was another son of Zeruiah? Joab. Abishai was the brother of Joab, and we know about him. Joab would call you aside and say, "Boy, you're my friend. Let's make a deal together." And then he would knife you in the back! (see 2 Sam. 3:24 *ff.*, 2 Sam. 14, 2 Sam. 18:9 *ff.*). We will not find anybody more bloodthirsty than Joab. The whole family was violent!

STEEL AND VELVET?

11 *Then David said to Abishai and to all his servants, "Behold my son who came out from me seeks my life; how much more now this Benjamite? Let him alone and let him curse, for the Lord has told him. 12 Perhaps the Lord will look on my affliction and return good to me instead of his cursing this day." 13 So David and his men went on the way; and Shimei went along the hillside parallel with him and as he went he cursed, and cast stones and threw dust at him* (NASB).

What a picture! Here is David running, fleeing, with his dedicated little army around him. Here is this *misfit*, this crazy man, Shimei, throwing dirt and rocks and stones, cursing him and accusing him of all sorts of untruths. And David seemingly floats through the midst of it all! Why, I look at David and say, "You have the hide of a rhinoceros." David was thick skinned! Many Christian people have skin which is too thin! We begin something for God in leadership: to step out for him, to teach a class, to bear a witness in the business world. And there is always some Shimei who will come and offer a discouraging word or criticism or question. He urges us to be careful or questions our judgement, and we surrender immediately. The devil knows how to abuse us, to lead us away from God, or to keep us from being effective in leadership in any walk of life because our skin is too thin.

Some of us need to say, "Lord, give me a thicker skin, the hide of a rhinoceros!" Have you ever really looked at a rhinoceros? A friend of mine has an exotic ranch. Once I was riding through the area in a little Jeep. And as I rounded a curve, there were two rhinoceroses, as big as Dallas! I believe a Sherman tank could go head-on with one of those giants and the tank would lose! I have never sensed such power in any kind of animal! Immediately I thought, "I know now why I have never heard of rhinoceros boots! Elephant boots, snakeskin boots, eel, but I have never seen a pair of rhinoceros boots. Their skin is too thick! Many people need skin like those rhinos.

But as our skins get thick, we must keep our hearts tender. Thick skin—tender, soft, compassionate heart. David must have had that combination. David said to Abishai and his men, "Well, evidently God is speaking through him, and I'm going to listen to whatever he says." That is really something!

Carl Sandburg spoke of Abraham Lincoln, "He's a man of steel and velvet." That type of person is a leader. The Christian man or woman who has a compassionate heart and skin which is thick enough to stay on the track is far ahead of the game.

GO WITH A WINNER

Then something happens. In 2 Samuel 19, we encounter Shimei again, in a different setting. David's army, to the surprise of all, is victorious over Absalom's army. David is being reinstated as king, and all the tribes are coming back saying, "David, we were for you all the time!" They are getting on the winner's bandwagon. David goes back across the Jordan to get his household possessions and to return to the palace, and as he is going back over the river, he meets Shimei.

> 16 *Then Shimei the son of Gera, the Benjamite who was from Bahurim, hurried and came down with the men of Judah to meet King David. 17 And there were a thousand men of Benjamin with him, with Ziba the servant of the house of Saul, and his fifteen sons and his twenty servants with him; and they rushed to the Jordan before the king. Then they kept crossing the ford to bring over the king's household, and to do what was good in his sight. 18 And Shimei the son of Gera fell down before the king as he was about to cross the Jordan. 19 So he said to the king, "Let not my lord consider me guilty, nor remember what your servant did wrong on the day when my lord the king came out from Jerusalem, so that the king should take it to heart. 20 For your servant knows that I have sinned. Therefore, behold, I have come today, the first of all the house of Joseph, to go down to meet my lord the king* (NASB).

Now that David is king again, Shimei falls down before him. 21 *But Abishai the son of Zeruiah answered and said, "Should not Shimei be put to death for this, because he cursed the Lord's anointed?"* (Old Abishai doesn't give up! "You should have killed him months ago, and now you're king again. Surely you're going to kill him. Let me get at him!") 22 *David then said, "What have I to do with you, O sons of Zeruiah . . .* (What a family. They were the "hit men" of that day.) . . . *that you should this day be an adversary to me? Should any man be put to death in Israel today? For do I not know that I am king over Israel today?"* 23 *And the king said to Shimei, "You shall not die"* (NASB).

Those were the same words which Nathan spoke to David when he was forgiven after his sin. That David was something! He heard all of Shimei's former, abusive language and action as a word from God. He would not let Abishai harm him; he would not let Abishai's second counsel affect him. He said, "No, not on this day. He's forgiven."

Remember the list you made at the beginning of this chapter? Do you need to add a name to it? Has the Holy Spirit reminded you of something deep in your subconscious? Now what are you going to do with it? How do you forgive and forget? How do you make it right with these "Shimei's" who come into your life? (Maybe you are a "Shimei"! Are there people whom you need to approach and with whom you should get matters right?) Can you wait and say, "My day will come"?

GOD'S KIND OF FORGIVENESS

As a pastor, my primary function is to help us understand that we are to be submissive to the Bible, the Scriptures. Therefore, when somebody says to me, "I didn't like what you said," it makes no difference when I am accurately interpreting the Word of God. But when someone says, "I don't agree with how you interpreted the Word of God," I'll listen. When God speaks, we are to be submissive to His word. And *that* is what we need to understand! That is obedience! Those who are under the authority of Scripture will be blessed by God—always.

Whether we like it or not, the truth is that if we are to be forgiven by God, we must forgive. The Lord's Prayer states, *And forgive us our debts, as we also have forgiven our debtors* (Matt. 5:12, NASB). Some of us should not pray that prayer because we have this list!

Jesus gives us more information in Matt. 6:14 and 15: 14 *For if you forgive men for their transgressions, your heavenly Father will also forgive you.* 15 *But if you do not forgive men, then your Father will not forgive your transgressions* (NASB). He says that in the direct proportion in which we forgive others, God will forgive us. And, the direct proportion in which we do not forgive others, the Lord will not forgive us. So if we want the forgiveness of God, we must be forgiving.

There is nothing that can happen to us or to our loved ones which we are not called on to forgive totally! How do I know that? Because we are to forgive as God in Christ has forgiven us. There on Calvary's tree, on the cross, Jesus' shed blood wiped away *all* of our sins. There are no exceptions, there is nothing so heinous, so unlawful, so immoral, that He cannot forgive. Therefore, we are to forgive *every* offense which comes to us, if we are to know forgiveness for ourselves.

Ephesians 4:32 says, *And be ye kind one to another, tender-*

hearted, forgiving one another, even as God for Christ's sake hath forgiven you. Nobody can really forgive in his human power. Forgiveness takes divine power, the Spirit of Jesus Christ will give us the power to forgive.

What about David? He had a tender heart and the hide of a rhinoceros when he said that God must be speaking through Shimei. Later he said, "I forgive you, Shimei. I give you my oath." David forgave prior to the coming of Jesus Christ, before His shed blood on Calvary. How could David do it? We cannot forgive totally without the Spirit of Christ. How did David do it? Did he do it???

As I began the study of this topic, "How to Forgive an Enemy," I read two passages of Scripture: 2 Samuel 16 and 19. Some of the commentaries which I checked exalted David and said what a wonderfully forgiving person he was; what a tough skin and soft heart he had. When he was down, he was loving; when he was up, he was loving. I concurred and worked on the subject of the forgiving power of David. But I ran into a problem when I realized that total forgiveness comes only with the power of Christ. David did not have that yet; Christ had not come!

COMPLETE FORGIVENESS?

In my study Bible, I noticed by the name Shimei, a little reference: 1 Kings 2:8. I said, "Shimei? What's he doing over in Kings?" Then I read the passage in its context. Eight or nine years had gone by, and David was an old man. In accordance with a promise he gave Bathsheba, sealed by Nathan the prophet of God, Solomon had been anointed king. And David was giving instructions to his son in this beautiful passage. He tells Solomon to be faithful to the law, to be a king of integrity and a man of vision, to follow the commandments and to walk with God. Then David advises Solomon:

> 8 "And behold, there is with you Shimei the son of Gera, the Benjamite, of Bahurim; now it was he who cursed me with a violent curse on the day I went to Mahanaim. But when he came down to me at Jordan, I swore to him by the Lord saying, 'I will not put you to death with the sword.' 9 Now, therefore, do not let him go unpunished, for you are a wise man; and you will know what you ought to do to him, and you will bring his gray hair down to Sheol

with blood." 10 *Then David slept with his fathers and was buried in the city of David* (1 Kings 2:8-10, NASB).

David's last statement to Solomon before he died was, "You know what to do—kill Shimei!" And after some chicanery, in the next chapter we read where Solomon did exactly that! Evidently all of David's previous talk was merely pious show—political expediency, external religion. After all, he had nothing to gain by killing Shimei. He needed to keep his good reputation. Later, when he was in charge once more and Shimei came into the picture again, David thought, "Oh, I'll be benevolent. I'll just forgive him." And all the people, the Abishais, were so impressed with what a loving, kind, benevolent, gracious king they had. A man after God's own heart! While all the time down deep in David's heart, he could not forget old Shimei!

And the Holy Spirit said to me, "Look at your own life." Before I found this passage in 1 Kings, I would not have thought of anyone against whom I held a grudge, had any bitterness, or wanted revenge. But David could not forget what Shimei did to him—after nine years! And I fell to my knees and prayed, "O Lord, show me if there is a Shimei in my life." And the Holy Spirit began to peel back layers which I had not thought about since childhood: my immediate family, junior high, high school, and college relationships. Then I found myself making a new list of people I had not forgiven. If I had seen any of these people, I would have played the game: "It's good to see you. You look great. How's everything?" But if I had heard that any of those people had fallen into difficulty or were having a rough time, I would have said, "They're getting just what they deserve for the way they treated me."

HOW TO FORGIVE

Only the power of Jesus Christ gives us the ability to forgive totally and forget, to love truly, those who have cursed us, abused us, and have spoken all manner of evil against us falsely.

Corrie Ten Boom in her book, *The Hiding Place,* tells that after she was released from the concentration camp at Ravensbruck, she began telling around the world the story of forgiveness and of how God had spoken to her through the horror of her sister's plight. She preached forgiveness to large crowds all over Europe and America. Corrie said, "One day I was speaking in a church in Munich, Germany, about forgiveness and about God's second touch. I was trying to deal with the overwhelming guilt which the German people felt following that global conflict."

Following the message, she was shaking hands with the people. A man came up to her and called her prison number. She said, "For the first time in many, many years, I heard that number. I looked at the man and recognized him immediately as one of the S.S. guards at Ravensbruck, who had brutalized my sister and me." He had stood guard outside the shower when she was admitted.

The man said to her, "Since the war, I've become a Christian. And I have been looking for anybody who was in those camps so that I could ask their forgiveness. And you, Corrie, are the first person I've seen. Will you forgive me?"

"I closed my eyes and I wished for a moment that God would strike that devil dead. He extended his hand and said, 'Will you forgive me?' I tried to lift my hand, and I could not do it. Then, I closed my eyes and I said, 'Oh, Lord, help me.'" And Corrie said, "I had a fresh vision of the cross, and I heard the voice of Jesus say, 'Father, forgive them, for they know not what they do.'

"Oh, Father, I cannot forgive this man. Give me the forgiveness of Jesus Christ." She lifted up one hand, and she literally felt the power, the love, and the grace of Jesus Christ flow through that hand, and then through her body as she reached out and took the hand of that soldier. "Oh, my brother in Christ, I forgive you!"

Forgiveness is not cheap and easy. When there has been offense and thorns, great or small, and we say, "Oh, I forgive you." that is *never* forgiveness! Forgiveness comes only through suffering. All forgiveness has in it the blood of Christ if it is true forgiveness.

Remember your list? Take that list, guided by the Holy Spirit; ask for the strength and power of Jesus Christ to flow into your life. Then through his strength, forgive all those who have abused, accused, or offended you. And the Holy Spirit will erase your list and make it clean! It works: I know from personal experience.

14
God's Man Plays the Fool— Again!

2 Samuel 24 and 1 Chronicles 21

And David's heart smote him after that he had numbered the people (2 Sam. 24:10).

NOT OLDER BUT BETTER?

For a long time, I thought that the older a person grew, the better he would become. "Surely, when I am older this sin won't bother me anymore; I won't be tempted like that! Maybe, as the years go by, I'll approach perfection, maturity, sanctification.

If you thought about it you would never make that statement, but this subtle idea refuses to die. Then when you look at some people who have been around you see the matter from another point of view. In fact, the person in the realm of my acquaintance who is the best at chicanery and deceit happens to be in her seventies! The meanest person whose name I could call is now in his eighties!

The problem is that we are becoming more and more of what we are going to be in the future. This happens *unless* God comes and deals with us, and we let Him touch and heal, change and restore, that area which we never have let Him control. In 2 Samuel 24, we find that David continued to have problems as an old man because there was still a part of his life which was not the Lord's (1 Chron. 21 is the parallel passage).

David had been king for about four decades. He had a large

family; he had written most of the psalms; he was known as a man after God's own heart. He was the sweet singer of Israel and the shepherd/king. He was a great man, and a godly man, for the most part. But in his old age, he played the fool again. The Devil captured him in yet another snare. Isn't that something? I could not believe it! Surely this chapter belongs back in the earlier years of his life. Then I thought, *How in the world could a murderer and adulterer write Psalm 23? How could the man who penned that great confessional, Psalm 51, go back to the same slime which had gotten him into the low place before? How could that happen, especially after so many years had passed? Isn't there some sign of maturity and growth in the heart of David?*

Look at the scene: David had been victorious again over the Philistines. The old warrior-king had led the army as they fought in the area of Gath. He had helped the army kill the remainder of the family of Goliath. (Goliath had brothers, and the Scriptures tell us in 1 Chronicles 20 that they had six fingers on each hand and six toes on each foot. And, they were nine feet tall!)

A CENSUS

David had conquered an area stretching from Dan to Beer-sheba, the broadest territory he had ever controlled. We know that he had a garrison stationed in Damascus and that the Syrians were servants to the Israelites. The Edomites were conquered. We hear nothing about the Moabites. David was in control, as problems began once more! 1 *Again the anger of the Lord burned against Israel, and he incited David against them, saying, 'Go and count Israel and Judah.'* (2 Sam. 24:1)

First Chronicles 21:1 gives better insight into the situation: *Then Satan stood up against Israel and moved David to number Israel* (NASB).

This event reminds us of the conversation concerning Job. God said, "You know, Job's my special man." And the devil answered, "I *guess so.* You built a hedge around him. You protect him. You bless him. Remove that hedge, and let's see what kind of man Job is!" And the hedge was removed.

God had put a hedge around David, his anointed king. But David was not walking with God. We have no record of many psalms being written during that time. He was enjoying peace and prosperity in his old age and semi-retirement. He was "at ease in Zion," to use the biblical phrase. Then Satan came and tempted him to count the people. Bible scholars have a field day trying to understand what was wrong with that! All David did was count everybody! Moses was instructed to take a census of God's people. Why shouldn't David be allowed to do the same?

Some say that his was the sin of presumption. David had no instruction from God. He presumed upon what he should do. "Don't presume!" they say. Some speculate that this was a military census carried out by Joab and therefore all the people should not have been counted. They argue, "His sin was that he counted those who were under age. These young men should not have been called upon to bear arms." Others say that his sin was that of leading the nation of Israel to a divisive stance. The figures were reported in this way: . . . *there were in Israel eight hundred thousand valiant men . . . and the men of Judah were five hundred thousand men* (2 Sam. 24:9, NASB).

Some scholars believe that David wanted to see just how successful his blood relatives—his own tribe—were becoming and to see if they were strong enough to battle against the other ten tribes of Israel. Therefore, this partisan spirit of David was his sin.

Now, I don't think that any of these interpretations are correct in the light of Scripture. They sound good and they are fun to talk about. Some truth can be seen in each one. But when I read the account in 1 Corinthians and in 2 Samuel, the sin is obvious: David's sin was pride!

A PROUD LOOK

Never are we so vulnerable to the beguilement of Satan as when we are puffed up with our own importance! This is what had happened to David. Victory and success had drawn him away from God. He talked to God and he worshiped in a perfunctory way, but there was no reality of God in his life. Therefore, he said, "Let's go out and count all the people." Perhaps he was thinking about further military battles to enlarge his territory. Maybe he wanted to rule beyond Dan and Beersheba. He could conquer all

DAVID: AFTER GOD'S OWN HEART

the way to Cairo, then up to Damascus, and farther. The Bible tells us that at the time, *All* the nations of the world respected the power of Israel. His problem was ego!

Proverbs 6 lists seven things which God hates: six things He hates; the seventh, He despises. The list begins with "a proud look," literally "a proud eye." David took this census not to testify, "Here are God's people; look what God has done with us," but so he could boast, "Ah, these are my people! Look what I have done! Look at the victories I have accomplished!"

David reviewed the reports and calculated, "Over 6,000,000 people are under my rule. I am their absolute king!" Incidentally, the population of Israel at that time was approximately the population of Israel today.

David had two major problems which allowed pride to enter his life. First, he was not walking with God. Second, he was not accountable to anybody. Even his family did not have a close relationship with him. He was absolute and supreme. That is a precarious posture to be in! Every man and every woman needs to be accountable to somebody! All of us need that person who will be honest with us, who will talk with us, who will share with us, who will love us in spite of what we do!

It is hard for people who are natural-born leaders, who like to be free-wheeling and dictatorial, to be under a group or a person to whom they are accountable. David did not even think that he had to answer to God! David's sin in counting all the people was that he wanted to see how important and powerful he was; he wanted to see if he could expand his bounds.

ADVICE FROM A PAGAN

From 2 Samuel 24 (NIV)

Look who warned David!

> 2 So the king said to Joab and the army commanders with him, "Go throughout the tribes of Israel from Dan to Beersheba and enroll the fighting men, so that I may know how many there are." 3 But Joab replied to the king, "May the Lord your God multiply the troops a hundred times over, and may the eyes of my lord the king see it. But why does the lord the king want to do such a thing?"

Joab tried to reprimand David! Why, if there is a more bloodthirsty rascal in all the Bible than Joab, I do not know who it would be! His idea of solving problems was killing people. Joab, an ungodly man, the commander-in-chief of David's army, a person who did not want to answer even to David, said a word for God to the anointed king of his people. (And when Joab reluctantly followed David's orders, it took him nine months to do it!)

Matthew 6:22-23 tells us: 22 *"The lamp of the body is the eye; if therefore your eye is clear, your whole body will be full of light. 23 But if your eye is bad, your whole body will be full of darkness. If therefore the light that is in you is darkness, how great is the darkness!"* (NASB). Now what does that mean?

When a person who has known the light of God in Jesus Christ has to make a decision, and that light has grown dim, a pagan will have more common sense and will make a better decision than that Christian who is away from the Lord. That's a fact! If you are away from God in your business or social life, and must make a decision about your family, an outright pagan with some secular, common sense will have better discernment than the person who has known and moved away from the light of God.

A pagan will speak to us many times when God cannot get to us any other way. Perhaps the greatest sermon I ever heard was preached by an atheist. God used that person to say a simple word to me which led me to a fresh walk with God in Jesus Christ. God tried to use Joab, but David did not pay attention.

REMORSE AND REPENTANCE

After the census was ended, conviction came upon David's heart. 10 *David was conscience-stricken after he had counted the fighting men, and he said to the Lord, "I have sinned greatly in what I have done. Now, O Lord, I beg you, take away the guilt of your servant. I have done a very foolish thing"* (NIV).

The one thing we must remember about David is this: He knew how to repent! When we sin, we can rationalize and we can explain it away. We confess our sins with some sort of escape clause. Not so with David! "Lord, I have sinned greatly. I have missed the mark again. Lord, I've played the fool yet another time." The difference between a man of God and a man who is away from God is how sin affects his life.

Are you wondering whether you are saved or lost, whether you are a Christian or not? How do you deal with sin in your life? An ungodly person will run *from* God. He finds something wrong in the church, he does not read the Bible, he does not pray. When a godly person sins, he runs *to* God. He must have that relationship with the Father. He wants joy and peace. He wants to be able to sleep again!

11 *Before David got up the next morning . . .* God was dealing with David in the middle of the night. Now, Psalm 16:7 tells us: *I will praise the Lord, who counsels me; even at night my heart instructs me* (NIV). However, Psalm 6:6, perhaps penned by David at this very time, says: *I am worn out from groaning; all night long I flood my bed pillow with weeping and drench my couch with tears* (NIV). The next morning David was ready for God to judge the sin he had committed.

PUNISHMENT: DAVID'S CHOICE

11 *Before David got up the next morning, the word of the Lord had come to Gad the prophet, David's seer:* 12 *"Go and tell David; this is what the Lord says: I am giving you three options. Choose one of them for me to carry out against you."* 13 *So Gad went to David and said to him, "Shall there come upon you three years of famine in your land? Or three months of fleeing from your enemies while they pursue you? Or three days of plague in your land? Now then, think it over and decide how I should answer the one who sent me."* 14 *David said to Gad, "I am in deep distress. Let us fall into the hands of the Lord, for his mercy is great; but do not let me fall into the hands of men"* (NIV).

As far as I know, this is the only time in the Bible when God gave an option for the consequences of sin. David could choose war, famine or plague. And he said, "I'll take the plague. I will put myself at the mercy of God!"

Man is in charge of war, and David knew the capriciousness of his enemies. He did not know what would happen in times of war, as he ran from his enemies. If famine came, those who owned the land and controlled the grain would control the nation. He did not know what these men would do. But he knew that God would be in charge of plague. He chose God's mercy.

Notice how the punishment fits the sin. The angel came and destroyed 70,000—from Dan to Beersheba. What was the boundary given for the taking of the census? Dan to Beersheba. What was the reason for the pride of David and of the people? "Look how vast we are. Look how we've been multiplied. Look at the health of our families. Look at what we've accomplished. We can control our destiny!" A sin of pride! The judgment of God came and seventy thousand were killed, but not in three days: The period was shortened by the mercy of God.

This probably was the second greatest tragedy in the history of mankind. In the battle at Syracuse, over 100,000 Carthaginians were killed in a day. In Hiroshima, for example, 70,000 were killed or *missing* that first day. In Nagasaki, about 40,000 were killed or missing. Seventy thousand were killed from Dan to Beersheba!

17 *When David saw the angel who was striking down the people, he said to the Lord, "I am the one who has sinned and done wrong. These are but sheep. What have they done? Let your hand fall upon me and my family"* (NIV). David became an intercessor with God! The corresponding passage in 1 Chronicles tells us that David was dressed in sackcloth and ashes, with his feet, his face, and his body in the dust. He was not on a throne! Whatever causes us to have pride, or builds up our egos, God will usually take from us, or he will turn it into a cross. The people had turned their attention from their greatness and their vast numbers, and they were all down on their faces wailing, "Oh, God, have mercy. Is there any answer for my children? For my wife?" Death and disease were rampant.

David went before God in sackcloth and said, "Oh, God, have mercy. Kill me. Kill my family. Spare the people." And the Bible tells us that the angel's hand stopped before it reached Jerusalem. It stopped literally in front of the threshing floor of Araunah the Jebusite (v. 16).

WORSHIP COSTS!

18 *On that day Gad went to David and said to him, "Go up and build an altar to the Lord on the threshing floor of Araunah the*

DAVID: AFTER GOD'S OWN HEART

Jebusite." 19 *So David went up, as the Lord had commanded through Gad.* 20 *When Araunah looked and saw the king and his men coming toward him, he went down and bowed down before the king with his face to the ground.* 21 *Araunah said, "Why has my lord the king come to his servant?" "To buy your threshing floor," David answered, "so I can build an altar to the Lord, that the plague on the people may be stopped."* 22 *Araunah said to David, "Let my lord the king take whatever pleases him and offer it up. Here are oxen for the burnt offering, and here are threshing sledges and ox yokes for the wood.* 23 *O, King, Araunah gives all this to the king." Araunah also said to him, "May the Lord your God accept you."* 24 *But the king replied to Araunah, "No, I insist on paying you for it. I will not sacrifice to the Lord my God burnt offerings that cost me nothing"* (NIV).

The threshing floor of Araunah the Jebusite was located on Mount Moriah, where Abraham took Isaac to offer him in obedience to God. The angel stayed his hand, and Abraham instead offered the scapegoat, which was caught by his horns in the bushes, as a sacrifice. Abraham called this place *Jehovah-Jireh,* "The Lord will provide." Abraham went there in obedience. David went there years later because of disobedience; but in both cases the Lord provided. God said to David, "Build an altar." God had accepted David back to Himself.

In Genesis 4, we see the first reference to worship in the Bible. We know that God had accepted Abel, because he accepted Abel's offering. Never try to give an offering to God until first your life is acceptable to Him! For that reason the New Testament tells us not to bring our gifts to the altar when someone has something against us, or when we have a grudge against anyone. We must go and try to make the situation right so that our worship will be acceptable to God. Therefore, when God said, "David, go build that altar," He was saying, "David, I have forgiven you. You're right with me now. Get on your knees and recognize what I have given to you and my people. You did nothing for yourself! I worked through you by my providence and in accordance with my divine plan and will." And so David built that altar on the threshing floor.

The threshing floor of Araunah the Jebusite (a Gentile who probably converted to Judaism) was the place where God told

David, "I want you to see that the Temple is built." And in that place Solomon built the Temple. In that place, all across the years, the sacrificial system was followed. Animals were killed, and the blood sacrifices were offered. The burnt offering and the peace offering and the offering of the tabernacles were made in that very place: Mount Moriah—"The Lord will provide."

On the other side of that very same mount, Jesus Christ was crucified on Calvary, as His blood was shed to take away the sins of the world. All of these events happened on the threshing floor of Araunah the Jebusite. Isn't that something? God through his prophets and his servants put this plan together beautifully and perfectly.

Araunah offered David the wood and the animals for sacrifice. David said, "No, I will not offer to God that which cost me nothing." What are you giving to God that costs you something? If your faith costs you nothing, it is worth nothing! You waste your time in church, and you waste your time playing religious games. You should not be called "Christian." True faith costs—what? Everything!

Gifts to him must come from hearts of sacrifice! There will be no crown or throne unless, first, there is sacrifice. If you want to find your life, you must throw it away, and you lose it for his sake. Now, I do not totally understand this, but what little I have practiced, works.

There on the threshing floor of Araunah the Jebusite, they built an altar. And on that altar, they put horns, one at each corner. If anyone was being pursued, he could go to the altar and hold onto one of those horns, and no one could harm him. That was the place where God provided protection, salvation, and cleansing.

APPLICATION

What does all this mean to us personally? What does it mean to a church? God honors a body of Christ as long as that church walks on its knees! Through the years, I have heard thousands of stories: "God honored this church when we had that pastor. God was alive in that program. God was alive in our missionary activities. God was doing this. God was saying this." It seems as though God works in a church or in a denomination, and then he backs away. God blesses a church and it grows. Buildings are erected, new programs are begun, and everything is alive. Something happens, and the people say, "Well, we lost our pastor," or, "There was a division in the church." "God doesn't seem to be around. We've prayed, but his hand of blessing is no longer with us." What has happened?

This scripture shows us clearly: That church begins to be filled up with pride. People say, "Look at my church. Look at what I'm doing. Look how my choir sings. Look what we're doing in my class." We might say, "God's doing it. The Holy Spirit is leading," but the truth is: As God looks at our motives, he sees that we believe *we* are doing it.

This is a warning to any church God is using. As God gives a cup of great blessing, he enlarges the cup so it can hold his blessing, promise, hope, and love. It then becomes more difficult to find hands steady, strong, faithful, and humble enough to hold such a cup. God will not honor his church when ego and pride dominate. But the church which walks on its knees will continue to be blessed by him. Anytime a body of Christ gets puffed up with what they think they are, or have, or have done, God will withdraw his Spirit. And over that church we can write "Ichabod"—"Anathema." God wants to honor every church, but he cannot do it because of those who are in the Body!

The second application is for us personally. What are we leaning on? What are we proud of? What are we holding onto? Accomplishments? Homes? Family? Health? Some ability, skill, success, or mental prowess? Economic security? If you think "I'm in charge of my life, I've got my domain, Look what I'm doing"— beware! God owns everything. He can take the haughtiest person and bring them to their knees: "Oh, God, be merciful to me, a sinner. I'm nothing, and you're everything."

So, this is a warning to a church and a warning to a life. God says, "Don't play the fool. Give me the glory; give me the honor. Do you want to be great? Walk on your knees! The way you find your life is to lose it. He that will be great among you, let him become the servant of everybody else."

Growing old will not help! We must be spiritually on our faces before God, dressed in our sackcloth, saying, "Oh, Lord, I'm yours. Do with me just as you want. When you bless me, I praise you. When you give me problems, I praise you. When I fall, Lord, I rush directly to you, because I cannot bear to be away from my Father."

I recall a husband and wife who are now divorced. Mother will not admit that she was wrong; neither will Dad. Therefore, the children are growing up under the cloud of a lie, and they don't have a chance!

Talk of 70,000 dying does not mean much to us. However, when we multiply life after life from godless homes, the tragedy is greater than the pestilence which swept over Israel. It is sweeping over our land because we do not have *godly* homes and because *pride* has come to our nation, to our cities, to our churches, to our lives! And God cannot tolerate a haughty spirit!

My wife's father was an invalid for fourteen years. Residing in a wheelchair, he lived as a man of God! He had a twisted smile which was the result of many strokes. But when I visited him, I felt as though I had experienced a touch of heaven. His sister, Frances, came in one day and inquired, "Bud, how do you maintain your great spirit?"

In his faltering speech he haltingly replied, "Don't you remember that song we would sing as children? 'Spirit of the Living God, fall fresh on me. Break me, melt me, mold me, fill me. Spirit of the Living God, fall fresh on me.' Look at me. Here I am broken and melted." But also he exclaimed, "Molded and filled with Him!" Anyone whose life is molded by Christ can rejoice and testify, "The longer I serve Him, the sweeter He grows."

The longer I serve Him, the sweeter He grows;
The more that I love Him, more love He bestows;
Each day is like heaven, my heart overflows,
The longer I serve Him, the sweeter He grows![1]

1. From "The Longer I Serve Him, (The Sweeter He Grows)" by William J. Gaither. © Word Copyright 1965 by William J. Gaither/ASCAP. All rights reserved. International copyright secured. Used by permission of The Benson Company, Inc., Nashville.